# PARENTING 101

## ALL YOU NEED TO DO TO SUCCEED AS A PARENT

ANTHONY EKANEM

Made with ♥ on the Notion Press Platform
www.notionpress.com

# Contents

# Preface

Those of us who have children know how special they are in our lives and how we would not trade them for anything in the world or the world itself. However, sometimes you have certain things you need to do that you cannot take your child with you to do. A perfect example of this would be work or an interview. A simple solution to a problem like that is to enrol your child into some sort of childcare programme.

Today, it is important to be extremely cautious when selecting a childcare provider for your children. It can be very difficult to trust people we do not know, especially when it comes to taking care of a member of your family. I'm sure you have seen some of the shocking videos online or heard some of the stories on the news about abuse and neglect taking place in some childcare locations. This is a truly terrifying thought. However, there are steps you can take to help ensure the safety of your child.

There are many things you need to consider when choosing a childcare provider. You may not know where to start with this list of questions because it is quite long. That is okay because that is exactly what this book is for. The following six chapters will go over some of the most important questions to ask when choosing a childcare provider. Continue reading and ensure that your child receives the best care possible!

By nature, children are full of happiness and enjoyment in life. They live what they see and believe. However, children will inevitably feel afraid of something most of the time. Just like adults, children also struggle with some challenges that hinder them from making the most of their childhood.

Children need to deal with fears as they grow up. From entering a new school to taking a big shot to cope with a bully in school, they are facing intimidating situations from time to time.

Unfortunately, many parents don't care about their children seriously even when they display their fears. This is an incorrect parenting method, which could make a child suffer from panic attacks and depression. If you love your children, this is the last thing you do not want to happen to them, so make sure to give them the support they need whenever their fears take place.

Those who have children know exactly how much they mean to them. You would do anything for your child as long as it would make them happy in the end. You are always worried about them and want nothing but the best for them. One of the best places you can start to ensure your child has a bright future is to know the basics of healthy childcare and know what to look for in a childcare provider.

CHAPTER ONE

# Caring For a Newborn Baby (The Baby's First Year)

Caring for your child will naturally be one of your biggest concerns. There are more tips on immunization and care in the first year in subsequent chapters, but right now let us talk a little about how you can choose a good paediatrician for your baby. Here is what to look out for when choosing your paediatrician:

1. Find a doctor who has a nice personality and communication style. Finding a doctor that is patient and listens to all your concerns is very important. Try and start the search for selecting your paediatrician ahead of your baby's birth.

1. Ensure that the paediatrician's office has a good staff – remember that your baby will spend time with nurses, medical assistants, and other support staff. When going to the office see how the place is – the atmosphere and way staff dress can be indicators of the type of place it

is.

3. Does he or she come recommended? One of the best ways of finding a good paediatrician is by talking to someone who has had first-hand experience. Do you have close family or friends who have used a good paediatrician?

4. The location of the office may also be a factor – we live in busy and stressed times so if time is a factor, make sure that the paediatrician's office is fairly close by.

5. Ask Questions – this is the only way that you can "feel out" prospective doctors and see if their philosophies closely mirror your own.

6. What to Expect: Your first baby can be a daunting thought – not all the preparation in the world can probably ease the anxiety that can be felt but if it is any help even doctors and paediatricians get overwhelmed when they bring their firstborn home from the hospital.

Before we go onto the topic of caring for your baby we will talk a little bit about what the mother can come to expect the day after labour. First, the mother will probably expect an all-over pain derived from the stresses of labour. The arms and legs are likely to be sore.

One point to note is that although aching legs are normal it would be prudent to go to your doctor if you get symptoms of tenderness, warmth or pain in the calves – this can include swollen or red veins. This is important as these symptoms could indicate thrombophlebitis – a condition when veins become inflamed due to blood clots.

Pregnant women are more at risk of this condition because the vein walls tend to relax a little during pregnancy. You can greatly reduce the chances of thrombophlebitis by walking soon after your delivery.

Other symptoms of pregnancy include stretch marks (which usually fade a few months after birth, darkened areas of skin (the linea nigra and areola are common), and a line running from the belly button to the pubic bone.

Your mom may also notice some hair loss about three months after birth – this is due to the change in the level of hormones and can be expected to stop within a couple of months after starting. Now that we are aware of a few of the common issues that mothers face immediately after childbirth, let's go on to caring for your new baby.

**First Few Days**

The first few days home from the hospital are important for both the baby and the parents. As parents, you will have gone through an intense birth process that is unlike anything else you have ever experienced. As a new mother, you will be drained - both emotionally and physically. The father can often have feelings of being overwhelmed by the huge responsibility he now faces. There probably is not much anyone can say or do to help you fully prepare for what you are about to experience.

During your first days at home, it may be wise to limit the number of visitors that you welcome into your home because you'll need a lot of time to recover from the birth process. Other than your immediate family and good friends you might want to ask other friends to wait a week or two before they descend on you with gifts and want to hold the new baby.

New mothers will want to pay attention to the way that they feel so that those "baby blues" don't creep up and surprise them unexpectedly. It is normal to feel a bit out of sorts and sad for the first couple of weeks after giving birth. Your body is going through some major physical changes after the birth of your baby. Your hormones will be changing, and you likely will be feeling a lack of sleep.

It is important to remember that this is natural and to allow yourself a good amount of time to recover from this. If you find yourself feeling more and more depressed it is advised that you should discuss it with your doctor to see if you are suffering from "*postpartum depression*". Symptoms of postpartum depression include:

- Overwhelming feelings of sadness and depression accompanied by crying.

- Having little or no energy.

- Feelings of guilt and worthlessness.

- Having no interest in your baby or being overly concerned and worried about your baby.

- Weight gain accompanied by overeating or Weight loss accompanied by not eating.

- Insomnia or oversleeping.

If you do have postpartum depression, then there are a few ways that you can try to beat it:

- Try and get as much relaxation as possible. When the baby is asleep use this quiet time to get some rest yourself.

- Be more understanding with yourself and do not put yourself under too much pressure to "get back to normal". Ensure that your family is aware that you need help with housework and so on.

- Try to limit the time that you spend just alone – keep your mind and body relatively active (for example by taking short, pleasant walks).

- Get professional help if the depression seems to be ongoing.

- Discuss with other mothers their experiences after birth. You may find that your friends and family members also went through the same issues as you.

During the first few days at home, your family will be adjusting to the additional member of your family. If you have other children at home, you may be dealing with feelings of jealousy as the new baby takes centre stage. Make sure that you include your other children in the day-to-day activities that are part of the new baby's routine. Remember that you are trying to adjust to some huge changes in your life so allow yourself the understanding and care that you would give to family and friends in your situation.

**Breast Feeding**

It is a myth that bottle-feeds, and breastfeeding is equally good. Mother's milk is the best for the proper growth of the child. Certain nutrients in the mother's milk help the baby fight illnesses while also promoting brain development. Compared to breastfed babies, formula-fed babies are more prone to illnesses.

Ideally, you should start breastfeeding the child within 2 hours of its birth, but do not worry if for some reason you are not able to do so - many mothers feed their children after a few days because of some medical reasons and they turn out to be just fine. Apart from milk, avoid giving the child any water or pacifier because the child is still learning to breastfeed and things like the bottle nipple and pacifiers can confuse the baby while nursing because milk doesn't flow as fast as it does through bottles.

Do give the child enough time to breastfeed. Don't limit the time. It could frustrate the baby. An average of about 10 to 45 minutes can be taken by the baby to completely satisfy itself. So how should you hold your baby during breastfeeding The answer to this is that see to it that the gums of the baby are on top of the areola because there is a chance of the nipples becoming sore if the baby just chews on the nipple instead of taking in the areola. You can hold the baby in a cuddling position and feed it or you can lie on your side placing your baby facing you. Usually, when the baby has had enough milk it will let go of the nipple on its own, but the baby takes usually half an hour on each side.

## Mother's Nutrition During Breast Feeding

A breastfeeding mother needs to have a healthy and balanced diet. A variety of foods are required during this period including:

1. Get lots of vegetables and fruits – try and have an intake of 5 portions a day of fruit and veg.

2. For additional energy try and take in starch-rich foods such as bread, pasta, potatoes, pulses, and rice – this will

provide a good source of energy.

3. Foods such as whole meal bread, vegetables, pulses, cereals and pasta will provide fibre – women occasionally experience bowel problems after childbirth and an intake of fibre daily will help with this.

4. Proteins such as lean meat, fish, eggs, and poultry.

5. Try and get two portions of fish per week (including some oily fish). Do not exceed 2 portions of oily fish per week.

6. Dairies such as cheese, milk and yoghurt are excellent sources of calcium and should be included in a breastfeeding mother's diet.

Some doctors advise taking vitamin supplements such as Vitamin D (10 mcg per day). Your doctor will be able to advise which supplements will be right for you.

In addition to the above foods that you should eat, there are certain food types that you should steer clear of at this time. As above you should restrict your intake of oily fish to two portions per week, but you should also avoid eating more than one portion of swordfish, marlin or shark per week as these fish contain high levels of mercury. You should also be careful with your intake of caffeine and alcohol. Some breastfeeding babies indeed react to the foods that their mother has consumed.

Some doctors believe that it is wise to lay off peanuts during this stage as well – approximately 2% of the population is allergic to peanuts – however, your baby may have a higher chance of being allergic if the mother/father/

brothers/sisters have problems such as asthma, eczema or hay fever. If you believe your baby may be at risk due to these factors, it is worth consulting your doctor.

**Diaper Changing**

The things you would need for your baby's changing are:

- Diapers
- Diaper changing tables
- Mild baby powder
- Diaper rash ointments
- Cotton balls
- Baby wash cloths
- Changing pads
- Terry cloth towels
- Baby wipe warmers.
- You can use wither cloth diapers or plastic ones. Usually, for newborns, cloth diapers should be used.

Lay a fresh diaper on the changing table. Put your baby on the table with her tummy facing you. Then unfasten the soiled diaper and gently pull it out from beneath the baby while slightly raising the baby's legs.

Clean your baby's genitals and buttocks gently with baby wipes or cotton balls dipped in lukewarm water. Then thoroughly dry up the area. You can apply mild baby cream and cornstarch powder if wanted.

Then pull the clean diaper underneath the baby and properly fasten the tabs of the diaper. Most babies do get diaper rash at some point; do not be afraid or tense as it is very common in babies and will usually clear up soon. If your baby gets diaper rash on the genitals or her buttocks or thighs, make sure you change her very often and that every time you do the area is cleansed properly. Rash cream may be applied where appropriate. It might be good to leave the baby without the diaper as often as possible as this helps in keeping the baby's skin dry and helps heal the rash faster.

**Is Child Crying?**

Your child could be crying because of some reasons, the most common of them being hunger. The other reason is indigestion or colic pain. Gripe water is often a good solution for mild colic pain. Usually, babies swallow some air while feeding which makes them uncomfortable and therefore, they cry. So after every feed, it is good to carry the baby upright and pat it on his back gently till it burps. Below are a few more of the common causes of crying and how to deal with them:

Lack of comfort – a soiled nappy, or tight or irritable clothing can cause crying in some babies. Ensure that your baby's nappy is always clean and discover what clothing is most comfortable for her.

**Why is My Child Crying?**

Sudden temperature changes – some babies may cry when exposed to temperature changes, for example, while bathing or having their nappies changed.

Lack of attention – some babies will cry when they feel the need for reassurance. There is a need here to find the right balance (for example if you cuddle your baby when she cries in the dead of night she may come to expect this night after night).

Now that you know a few of the things that can cause your baby to cry let us go on and see how we can give her (and you) a beautiful night's sleep.

How to Give Your Baby a Nice Night's Sleep When a baby is born, she does not know what is night and what is day. In case you are reading this book in anticipation of your first child then (as if you didn't already know) you should expect to be woken up persistently, no matter what the time, for the first few weeks. Partly, this is because a baby's stomach carries a maximum of three to four hours' worth of nutrition. Hence every few hours she will be waking up and cry. Without wanting to sound cruel, you should whenever possible try and impose the fact that night is for sleep from very early on – this does not mean letting her cry when she needs attention but doing things in a way that gives her less attention than she would expect in the daytime (e.g. try and keep the lights off for instance.)

You can also try and make her nap a little less in the afternoon time as this will naturally tire her out more during the night time and help her sleep better.

Here are some very effective tips on helping your baby sleep far better. Did you know that a lot of adults with persistent sleep problems stem from the early development years of a child's life? Hence your child needs to associate sleep with a sense of restfulness and peace – and you can help create those conditions. Here are the tips that you can use to induce far better sleep for your baby:

When your baby naps during the day time use a well-lit area – this will help keep the naps shorter and may encourage him to sleep better at night.

Feed your baby more during the day – this will help him meet his needs during the night so that he is likely to sleep better.

Carry your baby more, particularly in the evenings as this keeps him relaxed which is likely to lead to a more restless transition to sleep.

Remain flexible – if the sleep routine you are trying does not seem to be working then do not be afraid to try something new. Be alert too – where do you notice your baby sleeping well? If there is a "special place" then try and make that her sleeping place.

Try and ensure your baby has a pleasant day – as odd as it may sound, the more peaceful your baby's day the greater the chance that your baby will also enjoy a good night's sleep. Does some research show that babies that are held more during the day sleep better at night – is there any way you can work this into your daily routine?

Depending on the baby, sometimes a warm bath and massage can lull babies into sleep at night. You do need to see if this is right for her as this method can make some babies more stimulated. Trial-and-error is the way to find out.

A blend of soothing stimuli can help your baby sleep better too. For instance, after a warm bath and massage, hugging your baby and then breastfeeding her is very soothing and can help bring the onset of sleep.

What your baby wears during sleep can also be a factor – babies in the early months are known to prefer sleeping slightly tighter (snugly wrapped in a nice baby blanket). If your baby is prone to allergies it may irritate her more during the night – when this is the case remember to use pure cotton sleepwear.

Try and minimise the chances of physical discomfort. Things such as having a peaceful and quiet environment, ensuring that her diapers are dry and comfortable and making sure that the air is free, or irritants are very important.

The room temperature can also have a significant impact on your baby's sleep. Apart from ensuring that the bed is suitably warm the best temperature for sleep is 70 degrees with 50% humidity.

You also need to decide exactly where your baby should be sleeping. Some parents insist that your baby sleeps in his crib in his room. Still, other parents want their babies in their bedrooms. Neither is right or wrong and there are advantages to both. If your baby sleeps in her room you will likely get more rest for yourself since you won't be disturbed by the snuffling and other sleeping noises that newborn babies make. Your baby may wake less often if she is in her room, but this is not always the case. If your baby is sleeping in the same room as you are, you might find it less disturbing and easy to be able to attend to your baby's needs right there.

If you not only have your baby in the same room as you but also in the same bed, you should be aware of some of the dangers of sleeping in the same bed together. Baby experts are completely divided over the issue of sharing the same bed with your baby. You will have to research the safety versus the emotional issues and decide for yourself if you are going to be bringing your baby into bed with you.

You will likely need more sleep than your new baby. New babies most often are not able to sleep through the night until they have at least doubled their weight. This usually happens when your baby is between four and five months old.

CHAPTER TWO

# How to Help Your Children Overcome Challenges

The biggest challenge for most preschoolers and kindergartens is the thought of being separated from the things that are familiar, particularly their parents. Learn how to make the whole thing smoother and easier with the following ideas.

If it seems that your child is afraid to enter the school, he or she is probably thinking about being separated from you. You can handle it by taking the child to the school for a visit and doing it a couple of times before the start of the school year. Organize a tour, participate in some school events, and let them use the playground. Each time a child visits his new school and goes wearing a smile on his face and looks at you smiling, he is getting the message, saying that he could be happy while being there.

When your child still stays with you like a fastener when the class session goes on, you must make morning habits predictable, while making goodbyes short. Once you leave, the teacher may have your child distracted by letting him participate in the activity he loves. Placing a note on his lunch box or even a huge heart is good for nonreaders. Or perhaps, give him a seashell or "magic" acorn to keep inside his pocket and tell him that he will know that you are thinking about him each time he touches it.

When your child displays anxiety with bathrooms then you should find out the reason behind that. He is afraid maybe because he worries about not having enough time to get there. Does he feel scared of toilets as they flush fast? Is there a scary experience wherein his classmate crawls beneath the stand door? Open his fears, and then determine and discuss some techniques he can use to deal with them. You can also ask his teacher the time when the restroom is most quiet and let her tell your child to go during those times.

When making your visit, you can recommend visual cues, which could aid your child in navigating the school by him alone. Let him go around, including the bathroom area, and then show him the school's floors. A lot of buildings contain varied tiles or carpeting on every corridor or level. Discuss with the teacher something about the rooms which your child needs to get into during school days. After which, you can organize a map or make a shoe-box model to aid her in knowing more about the surrounding area.

The teacher is another factor that concerns many children entering the school. So, you should work on this too. As the first day of school approaches, many young students visualize a "child-crunching" monster who sits behind the desk of the teacher, particularly when older siblings teased them with such exaggerated stories. Before the school year starts, you may introduce your child to the teacher, and let him think of your relatives or any family friends who are also teachers.

Once the school year begins, your child might also think of his teacher as someone new when she differently does things from his daycare provider. It offers you the perfect chance to discuss classroom rules and the way people perform things in their unique ways.

Children by nature are good learners. You only need to make things easier for him to understand and learn. The fact that he feels scared about being at school should be addressed correctly and properly to allow him to go through and deal with the challenges successfully. This should eventually make you a better parent for him. So, make sure to keep these pointers in mind when looking to enrol your child on a school new to him.

**Stop Children Aggression**

Sometimes, some children become aggressive for an unknown reason. They hit, bite, push, and shove, which leads to hurting other people. You don't want your child to keep up with this behaviour, so knowing how to stop it today should be a good help.

Parenting is never easy, and parents are all humans. Each time your child expresses himself in a rebellious way, you are feeling much stress. Talking about this matter should be a great help for parents facing openly insolent children or when coping with aggressive kids.

This is not an easy thing to deal with and it is simply easier said than done in several cases. However, the little methods disclosed in this chapter should help you stay calm and cool whenever your child pushes those alert buttons. These methods are as follows:

- ***Count to Ten***. This might sound funny, yet it works wonders. Allow your child to see this as you do it. As you do the counting, take deep slow breaths. In addition, image yourself as calm, while going through the scenario with good results.

- ***Show Some Authority***. Determine that nobody has true authority over you except when you allow them. Furthermore, it is your choice to get upset or angry. Keep yourself reminded that if you give away more power, your insolent child will have less power to take from you. There is nobody else, but you will hold the key to your actions.

- ***Always Monitor Your Progress***. Create a list of the incidents wherein you have been successful when coping with the aggressive behaviour of children. And then, if you seem to falter, just keep yourself reminded of the good times when you've prevailed and gotten the best of the situation.

- ***Tell Yourself that It Won't Last Long***. Always remind yourself that it won't last more than a couple of moments. Think that it will simply pass and that nothing would last forever. And, your child will eventually grow up, whether defiant or aggressive, more likely quicker than you like them to.

- ***Feel Good for Being Responsible***. Keep yourself reminded of how good it feels to take responsibility for your emotional reactions. Give yourself some time for positive thoughts and feelings.

- ***Always Take Things Positively***. Consider the idea that someone else always takes it more difficult than you and that your experience can't be compared to what somebody else may have. Remember that the greater trial, the more fulfilling and greater the triumph would feel. Make use of it as your motivation until you get there, and eventually, you will.

- ***Don't Respond to Aggression with Aggression.*** Keep in mind that responding to aggressive behaviour with another aggressive behaviour is never a good idea. This will just validate and enforce the behaviour of the child. Your child desperately wants to become just like you and he or she would imitate any attitude you show.

- ***Become An Example.*** If you want to teach your child good behaviours, you will need to practice the things you preach to guide his misbehaviour effectively in the correct direction. Always teach and show your capability to manage your emotions. Keep in mind that the spotlight strikes you. Hence, each time you feel enticed to curse or yell, stop, and then reconsider that line of thinking.

- ***Teach Your Child the Alternatives.*** Show and teach your child some alternative techniques to manage his emotions. Provide approaches that are more constructive and more positive. Let him learn the ways to direct his emotions with creative expression. Encourage him to inform you whenever he feels upset or angry when possible.

- ***Recognize Their Efforts Consistently.*** Providing children with some reason to like changing is normally as simple as sharing affirmative recognition. No matter what, always remember that every child demands attention. Bad attention is quite better than totally no attention. Always provide your support and apply positive encouragement with your efforts whenever possible. All those methods mixed with positive encouragement should aid you in shaping an aggressive child into a more controlled and developed person.

These tips mentioned above are only a few of the many ways that you can use to stay composure when coping with aggressive kids. You have all the capability to stay calm when coping with aggressive kids and what it only takes is to know the best ways to respond in advance. When it comes to parenting, you will certainly appreciate the outcome of using the most applicable information available for dealing with misbehaving children. It doesn't need to be very hard, as all you require is some fresh perspectives.

**Control Your Children's Anger**

Just about every child feels angry seldom, yet when angry, negative comments and aggressive acts become a norm. Parents must do the right action to aid their children. Parents may help their children learn to deal with their emotions and display anger in the proper ways. Learn how to make it happen in this chapter.

**Anger Management among Children**

A lot of child behaviour issues focus on kids struggling with anger management. Disrespect, conflict, aggression, and oppositional behaviour may normally be alleviated by helping your kids know better handling of their anger. Once you teach your child with effective anger management skills, this will develop behaviour, while providing him one of the most essential life skills.

If you want your child to become a better person, teaching him how to better manage his anger is important.

Start today by considering the following pointers:

***Distinguish Between Behaviour and Feelings***

Normally, children face difficulty in knowing and understanding the distinction between aggressive behaviour and feelings. Let your child know about feelings, allowing them to learn to verbalize feelings of disappointment, frustration, and anger. Feelings, such as hurt, and sadness are covered by aggressive behaviours. Teach the child how to determine and verbalize his feelings rather than acting them out.

Furthermore, mention that feeling angry is fine. Anger is like some other emotions. Just know the right times when to feel it. Considering this will help children understand that discussing anger and feeling angry is not bad.

***Mould Proper Anger Management Skills***

You need to become a role model of appropriate behaviours, teaching them the better management of their anger. When your child sees you losing control, he will be more likely to experience trouble dealing with his anger or distinguishing what's right from wrong.

There are times when parents choose to hide their frustrations and feelings from their children. Even though it is right to protect children from adult issues, they also must witness just how you manage your feeling of anger. Produce chances to discuss feelings and allocate the right ways to cope with them. Citing some instances when you get frustrated can teach children how to discuss their feelings.

Be responsible for your behaviour, especially when you lose control in front of your kids. Say sorry and talk about what should be done instead.

***Implement Anger Rules***

When it comes to anger, most families preset informal family rules regarding acceptable and unacceptable behaviours. Other families do not mind slammed doors or raised voices, while some might have less acceptance for those behaviours. Make written home rules, which clarify to children the things they could do when they are angry and the kinds of behaviour that might lead to certain consequences.

Anger rules must focus on respectfully behaving towards others. Children must realize that only because they are angry does not give them the authority to hurt anybody. Deal with areas, like name calling, physical aggression and property destruction, so they know that they cannot throw and break things, or punt physically or verbally when they are mad.

***Educate Healthy Approaches to Manage Anger***

Children must be aware of the right way to cope with anger. Rather than simply telling, "Don't hurt your sister", say what they should do when feeling frustrated. Use time out as discipline rather than punishment. This way, kids will learn to take breaks by themselves, helping them to cool down.

Children may also take advantage of knowing some coping skills. Let them learn how to take breaks when they are frustrated. Demonstrate to them some relaxation techniques by doing some enjoyable activities. Furthermore, you may teach them some problem-solving skills, while helping them know how to resolve conflicts calmly. Most especially, tell them to walk out when they are angry to avoid being aggressive.

***Give Consequences When Needed***

Children demand positive consequences once they follow anger rules, while they need negative consequences once they break them. Positive consequences are particularly crucial for children, who normally face hardships with anger management. A token economy or reward system may offer an additional incentive to aid them to stay calm and apply their skills for managing their anger safely.

For any aggressive behaviour presented, there must be direct consequences. Based on the age of your child, consequences might include loss of privilege, time out or even restitution payment through performing additional chores or giving a toy to his victim.

It is just normal for children to have a hard time when managing their anger sometimes. However, this difficulty in anger management might result in some serious issues for some children in the long run. When the concern about the behaviours of your child or child's anger management issues grows, seeking professional assistance is recommended. A knowledgeable and skilled professional may rule out any fundamental psychological health concerns and may provide a behaviour or anger management plan.

**Give Your Children Good Nutrition**

To become better people, children need to be emotionally, mentally, and physically healthy. No parent would want her child to get sick, so making sure that he is healthy, especially physically, is important. Give your child the best nutrition to prevent sickness from taking place. You must know how, with the following ideas.

**A Healthy Body Is Away from Illness**

Nutrition for children is based on similar principles to adults' nutrition. Everyone requires similar kinds of nutrients, including minerals, protein, fat, carbohydrates, and vitamins. However, children have specific needs that should be sustained appropriately.

Feeding young children with a balanced diet could be very hard, specifically when he belongs to a group of fussy eaters. With this problem, you might feel worried that he might not get sufficient nutrients to grow and stay healthy.

A balanced diet contains an extensive range of foods, consumed in varied combinations daily. By eating a lot of different food items, a balanced diet may help to provide your child with all the vitamins and nutrients his body requires. It simply means that you need not worry about his lacking something important in his diet.

On the other hand, giving your child a balanced diet daily could be a bit of a challenge. Hence, try not to over think when you do not always attain it because provided that your child consumes well at most times, he would be gaining lots of nutrients he needs.

***Types of Food You Should Feed Your Child for a Balanced Diet***

The main idea to keep in mind is that you do not need to stick with a particular food item to help your child get some nutrients his body needs. For instance, meat would provide your child with protein, yet he may also acquire protein from chickpeas or nuts.

Furthermore, you may provide your child with primary nutrients in various forms. So, when he refuses a glass of milk and one boiled egg, you may instead try providing him with a pancake. Giving your child a range of foods would help in making the consumption a lot more exciting. Also, it encourages him to try different flavours.

To aid your child in eating well, provide him with a range of foods from the following food groups.

***Starchy Foods (Carbohydrates)***

Provide him with starchy foods in every meal and some snacks. These foods include:

- Cereals
- Rice
- Couscous
- Pasta
- Sweet potatoes and potatoes
- Plantains
- Yams

Foods made of flour, including bread and crackers, also belong to starchy foods. Your child might not appreciate starchy foods from wholegrain, so try providing a combination of non-wholegrain and wholegrain foods. Doing this would also prevent him from feeling excessively full of high-fibre foods to acquire a fine variety of nutrients. Keep in mind that your child has a tiny stomach, and it will be easy for him to feel full.

***Vegetables and Fruit***

Getting your child to consume a range of fruit, particularly vegetables could be challenging. Keep giving them to your child so that he knows that they are a typical part of the meal. You may also experiment with uncommon fruit, like star fruit, to keep the interest of the child. Or provide a plate of various-coloured fruit to lure him, including kiwi fruit, strawberries, banana, and blueberries. Try to always provide your toddler with fruit as part of his sweet meal.

***High-Protein and High-Iron Foods***

Your child must consume foods which are rich in protein and iron at least two times daily. Those food items that contain a lot of protein and iron are:

- Fish
- Meat
- Nuts
- Eggs
- Pulses (such as beans, lentils, and chickpeas)

Ensure that any products containing meat you purchase are high quality and are made from lean meat with a low quantity of additional salt. When you need to feed your child with nuts, you can grind them up and blend them into the meal. This should help in preventing him from choking. You may try to keep those foods interesting by experimenting with meat marinades and producing your hummus or lentil dhal.

***Dairy Foods***

You can give your child some dairy foods for times per day. Dairy products contain high calcium content that is essential for strong teeth and bones. These dairy foods can include:

- Milk
- Yoghurt
- Cheese

When feeding your child with yoghurt, choose the plain one or the type, which does not contain excessive sugar. To sweeten plain yoghurt, you may mix it with some pureed fruit.

For young children, milk is still a great source of calcium. Choose to provide your child with about 350ml of milk per day. It is good not to provide him with more than the amount because it would reduce his appetite for other foods.

Your child's health is important more than any other thing, so make sure to give him the highest wellness level he deserves by making a checklist of the food items mentioned above. By considering this, you will be able to aid your child in preventing sickness.

**Nutrition for Children**

Who doesn't love junk food? Almost everyone is craving the delicious taste of these ready-to-eat food items, which are loved by most children in several countries. However, parents should know that too much eating of junk food by their children might lead to an unhealthy lifestyle. Know how to replace junk foods with healthy snacks in this chapter.

**Getting Healthy Snacks over Junk Food**

Junk food pertains to any food item that contains low or no nutritional value. However, today, it seems that this type of food has already been consumed by lots of people of all ages, especially young children. You do not want junk foods to consume your child, so how exactly could you keep your child away from these unhealthy snacks?

As a parent, you know that junk foods won't make your children healthy, and it could be difficult to find ways to prevent their craving for them, as they are found everywhere. In this case, what you need is an effective alternative to junk food. Junk food has provided "snacking" a bad impression. Taking snacks between meals is never a bad idea, depending on your food choices though. So, if you want to give your child some healthy snacks, consider the following:

- ***Popcorn***– The fat within these microwave brands may be the mere negative here. You can go for healthier versions, having 98 per cent fat-free. When you choose plain popcorn, it is fine to sprinkle a bit of butter or margarine (no trans-fat). It is better than those full-fat brands in which you cannot control the added fat.

- ***Ice Cream***– Let's be real. Everyone knows ice cream is not a daily snack. However, there are some fine choices within the ice cream land. Breyer's Light Vanilla can be one of the best-tasting vanillas. In addition, fudge bars could be very delicious. They will suffice your ice cream and chocolate craving. Furthermore, they have 4g soluble fibre, roughly any fat, 80 calories, and extremely fine flavour.

- ***Fruit And Fruit Smoothies***– These are fine snack choices. For a sustainable, complete snack, you can produce some fruit smoothies for your child. The dairy should sustain you.

- ***Cookies***– This is a healthy choice for a snack. You can make some creative cookies that will lure your kids from trying some on their snacks. Cookies are something that kids will enjoy, put in some effort though.

- ***Crackers And Cheese***– This can be another great choice only when you choose a reduced-fat cheese, which tastes good. Reduced fat means a greater amount of protein. Crackers must be low-fat wholegrain for them to become a healthy snack. More fat contained in a cracker means more trans-fat it would contain.

- ***Frozen Yogurt/Yogurt***– If your child does not like drinking milk, yoghurt can be a great alternative source of calcium. Yoghurt does not require sugar to taste good.

Purchase plain yoghurt and complement it with something, such as fruit and low-fat granola, for a healthy snack.

- *Cereals*– This is a good choice for a healthy snack. But make sure to choose low-sugar, high-fibre cereals such as oatmeal.

- *Frozen Fruit/Popsicles Bars* – Another fine snack, these bars can be a great addition to your healthy junk food alternative. However, you must go for the right ones. There are a few excellent choices around, including the 100 per cent fruit-juice selections out there.

- *Candy Bars* – When you give your child the mini-sized ones and not the oversized ones, candy bars can be a fine choice. Do not deprive your child of eating something, as it will only lead them to compulsive overeating.

**Is Home School Good for Children?**

Sometimes, parents choose to let their kids attend home school rather than letting them attend normal school. But then, some parents wonder if homeschooling is good for kids or not. Know the reasons behind the following ideas in this chapter.

**Home Schooling: Is It a Good Choice?**

Parents may choose to teach their children for several reasons. Some of these reasons include the fact that they like to spend more bonding time with their children while establishing a more favourable relationship between them. A lot of parents may choose home schooling for their kids when they are unable to carry on with the standard curriculum.

The option for homeschooling depends on your child's unique situation. For instance, children with ADHD are more likely to experience writing trouble. With this, they may have problems dealing with their written tasks since they face difficulties with their planning. This option should enable them to do the tasks at their disposal. Parents of ADHD children attested that the option has eased them from stress. They customize lessons depending on the learning capabilities of their children. Since schools may overload their minds with unneeded information, parents who choose to home-school their kids could ensure that they teach their child in a way through which he or she can easily learn.

Furthermore, parents become apprehensive about schools' learning environments with their kids learning wrong or bad behaviour from other students. On the other hand, when home-schooled, kids might not just become better behaved the way their parents like, but also acquire the necessary education.

Experts suggest several good reasons why parents should instruct their children. With home schooling, parents will no longer need to aid their kids with tiresome homework as well as additional assignments.

To make the approach more effective, hiring an educational consultant may be a good idea. This consultant will help you out when dealing with the curriculum for home schooling your child. She will monitor your child's progress. There are times when families could have mixed meetings and scheduled play dates for the kids in the office of the consultant.

Moreover, you may also check some online information provided by the local authorities, helping you with successful home schooling for your child. Home schooling could become a fulfilling and enjoyable experience with the right methods and assistance at hand. Don't forget to mix your parent's love and care with the ingredients to make it more successful.

**Does Your Child Have ADHD?**

A lot of parents are afraid of finding out that their child has ADHD. Different from other disorders and problems, ADHD is a condition that bears both social and psychological impacts on just about anyone related to the child. Learn how to determine if your child has one.

**Identifying ADHD in Children**

ADHD, which stands for Attention Deficit Hyperactivity Disorder, is considered a neurological disorder. The condition is characterized by hyperactivity, mood swings, and forgetfulness. Not only children but even adults could be affected by the disorder, with as many as 5-8 per cent of children suffering from this condition, while many go undiagnosed every year.

**What Is ADHD?**

ADHD is a disorder in which the sufferer finds himself distracted, oblivious of what is happening around him, or extremely active in doing his activities. Most of the cases among children are developed before reaching the age of seven. Its diagnosis might come when there are issues with their development. For instance, they might display behaviour, which is wrong in attention or might become very impulsive, leading the condition to other issues.

Common places where this could be observed include education, peer and family relations, in social and occupational skills. When your child has insufficiency within these areas, it is recommended to seek some professional assistance, such as a paediatrician.

**Symptoms**

There are 3 kinds of ADHD, namely predominantly hyperactive-impulsive, inattentive and the combined type. The following are a few ADHD symptoms:

- Destructiveness
- Restlessness
- Impulsive behaviour includes too much talking, interrupting others, and blurting out the answer before a question should be answered. In addition, people suffering from this condition normally feel the desire to speak what's on their minds, which typically comes with creating statements without considering their consequences.
- Inattentiveness could be both a hardship with persistence to activities and sustaining attention.
- Hyperactivity occurs mostly in middle and early school-age children and it normally reduces as they grow.
- Difficulty in re-engaging in a recent task is evident as well.
- In adulthood, it could include restlessness and the need to remain busy physically is obvious.

For children, who have predominantly inattentive kind of ADHD, symptoms may include:

- Sluggish behaviour

- Confused behaviour
- Staring frequently
- Hypo active
- Daydreaming

ADHD can be a serious issue that parents should immediately address. So, if you suspect that your child might be having one, do not think twice and bring him immediately to a medical professional, who can suggest ways how to effectively deal with the problem. Early diagnosis means early treatment, so make sure to make the right decision today!

CHAPTER THREE

# Childhood Nutrition

Getting your child or a child that you are looking after to eat healthy can seem like a somewhat impossible task. Children can be very picky at times and for the most part, vegetables and other healthy foods are not high on their list of preferences. The good news is that it is possible to get your child to eat healthy nutritious food and you can even get them to like it.

A lot of the process of getting your child to eat healthy is a trial and error-process. You are going to have to keep trying new things and preparing them in different ways until you become familiar with what healthy things your child does and does not like.

There are a lot of tips and tricks you can use to get your child to eat healthy, many parents just are not aware of them. You should use as many of these tricks as you can because proper childhood nutrition is extremely important for the development of a child. Children who are malnourished in their earlier years will have noticeable health problems in the future and may suffer from certain deficiencies such as anaemia. I am sure you do not want your child to have to go through something like this so get them eating healthy!

Childhood nutrition is highly important for the healthy development of a child. The sad thing is that a lot of children are malnourished in today's world and many of them go to bed hungry at night. At the same time, there are children all around that are obese and their health is beginning to show evidence.

As mentioned before, proper nutrition is very important for any person but this is especially true when it comes to childhood nutrition. This is because the food that your child consumes today will have a direct impact on their growth and their health throughout their adolescent and adult years. This can either be a negative or a positive impact, depending on what the child is consuming.

If you want your child to grow up to be big and strong and also have excellent health, you need to do your part as a parent and make sure that your child is getting all of the nutrients that they need. This task can be somewhat difficult at times but it is important that you remain determined and persistent.

**Nutrition Basics**

It is very important that you are aware of how important proper nutrition is as a parent and that you are knowledgeable on how to properly give your child nutrients.

If you do not help your child by steering them towards healthier eating habits they will surely have negative effects on their health that you will notice later in life. Providing your child with well-balanced nutritional meals will help to prevent certain eating disorders and other issues such as anaemia or obesity.

The following are some examples of why proper nutrition is so important:

**Childhood Obesity Prevention**

As mentioned before, it is extremely important to make sure that your child eats healthy food that is full of nutrients, especially in their earlier years. That is why it is so shocking that roughly twenty-five per cent of children in the United States that are between the ages of two and eighteen years old meet the criteria to class them as being overweight. That is quite a bit of overweight children. It may be hard for you to believe but that fact comes straight from the CDC so start believing! The scary thing is the fact that overweight and obese children have a much greater risk of developing health problems later on in their lives. They will be at risk for joint issues and pain. As well, they will be at risk of getting serious problems such as cardiovascular disease or type-2 diabetes. Teaching your child at an early age to eat healthy and choose a piece of fruit over a candy bar will greatly reduce their risk of experiencing these problems.

**Healthy Growth**

Optimal nutrition is vital for a child to grow healthy. It is important to make sure that your child is consuming the proper amounts of nutrient-dense food such as fruits and vegetables to support optimal growth. Calcium is also very important. This nutrient will ensure that your child grows up to have fully developed and strong bones. Calcium deficiencies can have some undesired effects on your child's health so you want to make sure that you are giving your child adequate amounts of calcium.

**Nutritional Breakfast**

You must make sure that your child has a nutritional breakfast every day, especially on days that they have school. Studies show that children who have a nutritional breakfast before class do much better and can focus and participate much more. An interesting fact is that children who do not have breakfast or have an unhealthy breakfast are much more likely to have behavioural issues and problems learning while in school. On the other hand, well-nourished children are much more likely to have better memory and problem-solving skills.

**Consequences of Improper Nutrition**

As mentioned before, proper nutrition is extremely important for a child, especially in their earlier years. If a child does not consume the proper nutrients they will surely face certain issues in the years to come of their life. For example, a lack of proper nutrition as a child can lead to problems such as having a shorter or slumped-over stature. Another issue that these children may face is a delay in reaching puberty and this can have a serious impact on the rest of their life. As well, children who are not receiving proper nutrition are at risk of becoming dehydrated or facing certain health issues such as anaemia. Their academic performance will likely be affected and this also can have lasting consequences on their life. Then there is always the fact that your child might become over-weight or obese. This can cause the child to experience serious health and social problems in life.

You as the parent must make sure that your child is getting all the nutrition that they need. Your child counts on you to keep them safe, and making sure that your child is eating right is part of keeping them safe. The best part is that if you teach your child at an early age to eat healthy, they will likely continue to eat healthy, even when they are grown and have moved out. It may be a bit challenging at first to prepare healthy meals and get your child to eat them but it will get easier with practice and as you become more familiar with what healthy foods your child likes and what healthy foods they do not like.

**Important Nutrients for Children**

There are certain nutrients and different types of vitamins that are very important for a child when it comes to their development. This is true for the health of all people and not just that of children. The truth, however, is that a lot of people are not aware of how important these nutrients are or exactly what types of nutrients they should be looking for in their food when making meals for their children.

Most children who are lacking in nutrients are usually lacking the same minerals and vitamins and other forms of nutrients. The lack of these nutrients may not present any immediately noticeable effects on the child's health, but eventually, it will take its toll.

The following paragraphs will go over what nutrients children are commonly missing and will also provide you with some examples of ways in which you can incorporate these nutrients into your child's diet.

**Commonly Overlooked Nutrients**

Many people, especially doctors and others in the medical field, would agree that far too many children are consuming too many calories and not enough healthy foods such as whole grains, fruits and vegetables. This is exactly what is contributing to the problem of childhood obesity in the Unites States. You must begin teaching your child from a young age to eat healthy and to consume all of the nutrients they need to maintain good health and be strong.

Some forms of nutrients are more common to be missing from a child's diet than others. The following are some examples of these nutrients:

**Calcium**

Many children do not have enough calcium in their diet. The problem with this is the fact that calcium contributed to children developing strong bones. New research also suggests that there are many other benefits from calcium that were previously unknown. For example, it is now believed that calcium can prevent breast cancer as well as other forms of cancer. As well, calcium is now believed to help protect your heart and arteries. Given the current high rate of heart issues and breast cancer, we should be doing everything that we can as parents to help ensure that our children will not have to go through health issues such as these later in life. One way that you can get your child to start consuming more calcium would be to have them eat a bowl of fortified cereal with breakfast. Do not use whole milk for the cereal. Also, you may want to consider sending them to school with yoghurt for a snack.

**Vitamin D**

Vitamin D is another form of nutrient that is extremely important for the growth of healthy and strong bones. Vitamin D is absorbed through the skin and it is provided by sunlight. The thing is that children seem to be spending less and less time playing outside and more and more time sitting on the couch watching TV. Limit the amount of time that your child can play video games or watch TV each day and this will surely contribute to their getting out in the sun much more often. There are other ways you can get vitamin D other than the sun. A few examples would be rockfish, tuna, or vitamin D fortified milk.

**Potassium**

Potassium is a very important part of anyone's diet, but this is especially true when it comes to the diet of a child. It is a little-known fact but a lack of potassium in a diet can result in high blood pressure and other undesired medical issues. You need to make sure that your child is consuming enough potassium because it is extremely important.

Potassium can be found in many different types of food. A few examples would include beans, spinach, potatoes, and tomatoes. Tasty fruits such as bananas also contain high amounts of potassium.

**Fiber**

Many people are not aware of just how important fibre is in their child's diet. Consuming the proper amounts of fibre daily is a great way of preventing certain issues such as heart disease and type-2 diabetes. Fibre is an indigestible part of plants that we eat in our food. It helps digestion and other parts of your health. You can give your child a lot of fruit or vegetables to help them get the right amount of fibre or you can try feeding them nuts or cooked dry beans.

**Vitamin A**

Making sure that your child gets enough vitamin A is very important for many different reasons, however, many children are still lacking when it comes to the intake of this vitamin. The problem with this is the fact that vitamin A contributes to healthy eyesight. Vitamin A also contributes to a healthy immune system and is also involved with tissue growth. I am sure that you do not want your child to have to wear bottle-thick lenses on their glasses by the time they are in their teens so make sure they are getting enough vitamin A. You can get your child to consume more vitamin A by feeding them food such as sweet potatoes, and romaine lettuce, as well as dark and bright-coloured vegetables.

**Teach Your Children to Eat Healthy**

Your child must know how important it is to eat healthy food and that they are aware of what types of food are healthy and what types of nutrients are important. It is also very important that your child is aware of what foods are unhealthy and what types of food they should eat in moderation.

Everyone deserves a sweet treat from time to time but it is important to know how to limit these treats and not make them a part of your child's diet. The duty of teaching a child how to eat properly falls on the parent. You must know you need to teach your child to eat properly and that it is nobody else's job but yours.

You must teach your child about the importance of proper nutrition. It is also highly important that you inform them of the dangers and negative impacts of not eating healthy can have on their life.

**Be a Good Example**

You need to teach your child to eat healthy food and you need to start teaching them these things from a very early age.

One of the best ways to teach your child to be healthy would be to set an example and eat healthy foods yourself. Think about it, your child follows everything you do and uses you as their example for what you are supposed to do and how you are supposed to act in life. Therefore, if you set your child a positive example and make sure that you eat a healthy diet they will almost surely follow suit and see it as a normal thing to eat healthy foods.

Another good way to teach your children about the importance of proper nutrition is to learn how to limit the number of sugary treats and other types of unhealthy snacks that you introduce into their diet. Make sure that your child knows that it is fine to have an occasional candy bar but make sure that they also know that it is not a good idea to eat one every day.

Try to keep more healthy drinks around the house as opposed to having an endless supply of soda. Raising your child to enjoy healthy food will likely lead to their continuing those eating habits throughout their life. On the other hand, raising your child to enjoy unhealthy food will also likely result in your child continuing those eating habits throughout life.

As mentioned before, teaching your child to eat properly and to have a nutritional diet is extremely important for the development of a child. It is best to start this process as soon as possible because children absorb information like a sponge, especially in their earlier years.

**Optimal Nutrition for Children**

I am sure that after learning all of the previous information regarding nutrition and how important it is for your child, you are wondering how you can go about making sure that you are providing your child with these nutrients. As mentioned before, many people are completely unaware of what foods contain what nutrients. If you are one of these people do not be embarrassed because it is quite common. It has become a habit for our society to worry more about what tastes and smells good when it comes to food and not the nutrients that the food contains.

You must have your child on a diet that consists of proper nutrition. If you are unsure of what foods contain what nutrients and what the best types of food to feed your child are, you are in luck because the next paragraphs are just for you.

The following chapter will go over optimal nutrition and will provide you with some examples of types of food that you can feed your children to ensure they are getting proper nutrition.

**Healthy Food for Optimal Nutrition**

There are a lot of different types of food that are available that are packed full of nutrients and are very healthy to eat. The problem is that you are going to have to find a way to eat these healthier foods over your favourite snacks that are on the unhealthy side. Sometimes it may feel like this process will be impossible, but it is possible and it is not that hard if you go about it in the right way.

There is a lot of healthy food that is quite appealing when it comes to the way it looks and smells. A lot of the process of trying to get your child to eat healthier food will be trying to find healthy food that he or she likes.

The following are some examples of different types of healthy food that you can feed your child:

**Eggs**

Eggs are very healthy and make a great breakfast. They are packed with protein which is very important to have in your child's diet. They also contain many other nutrients, one of which is vitamin D. If you remember, we discussed earlier that vitamin D is important for your eyesight as well as your immune system. One of the best things about eggs is that most people like them, especially children. This will make it much easier to get your child to eat something healthy. Try making cool designs or funny faces with the eggs as this will also help to get your child to eat them.

**Oatmeal**

Oatmeal is another healthy food that you should not have a hard time getting your child to eat. Oatmeal contains high amounts of fibre-rich whole grains. Oatmeal is digested slowly which will also give your child a steady stream of energy to get them through their day. This will allow your child to find it much easier to concentrate and participate while at school.

**Fruits**

Having your child eat fruit is always a good idea. No matter what type of fruit it is, it is guaranteed to be full of vitamins and minerals. As well, your child will consume fibre while eating fruit and this is very important for their digestive system. Try to have your children eat a variety of different fruits as this will have more of a nutritional effect.

**Nuts**

Nuts are very nutritional and can be very good for your child to consume. You can get protein from nuts as well as other essential vitamins. Also, nuts offer a healthy source of fat and this is extremely important in a child's diet because they will need it to allow proper growth. As well, the fat provided by the nuts will give your child the energy they need to remain productive throughout the day.

**Milk**

Milk is always important to incorporate into a diet; this is especially true when it comes to children. The good thing about milk is the fact that it should not be difficult for you to get your child to consume it. There are many different ways that your child can consume milk besides just drinking it. Be creative with it and your child should have no problem-consuming milk.

**Tomatoes**

A sad fact is that it seems as if the cancer rate around the world continues to climb higher and higher as time goes by. The good thing is that there are certain types of food that you can give your child that will help prevent them from getting serious illnesses such as cancer. Tomatoes are an example of this type of food. This is because tomatoes contain something called lycopene. Lycopene is believed to fight off certain types of cancer. Cooking the tomatoes is even better because the heat will cause the tomatoes to release even more lycopene which will make them even healthier for your child to eat.

**Mealtime for Your Children**

Many people and parents are unaware of the fact that it is not only what your child eats that contributes to their eating healthy but also the environment and eating habits that your family has as a whole.

Meal time is very important and it should not be spent in front of the TV. Meal times are a chance for bonding, and believe it or not they offer a perfect opportunity to teach your children the importance of eating healthy food.

The following paragraphs will go over the importance of eating meals as a family and will provide you with some examples of how exactly you can use mealtimes to influence your child to eat healthier food.

**Use Mealtimes to Provide Examples**

Mealtimes provide parents with a great opportunity to communicate with their child or children. This time can be used as an opportunity to talk to your children about the importance of eating healthy foods as well as provide them with some examples of things that could happen to them if they do not eat healthy food.

The following are some examples of how and why eating as a family can encourage healthy eating habits that will be sure to keep your child well-nourished.

**Parents are Examples**

As mentioned before in this book, your child looks up to you for guidance in everything you do, including the food that you choose to eat. If your child sees you eating healthy food regularly, they will be much more likely to eat healthy food as you set an example for them.

**Children are Different**

If you have more than one child, you are probably more than aware of the fact that children like and dislike different things. For this reason, you need to understand that your child may not like the same healthy foods as one of your other children. You will need to determine what each of your children's likes and dislikes are and use this information during meal planning.

**Social Interaction**

The social interaction that is provided by eating meals as a family can contribute to a child having healthier eating habits for many different reasons. One of the most beneficial reasons is probably the fact that eating as a family and having conversations as a family will force your child to slow down with their eating. This will help your child better determine when they are full and this will help your child refrain from over eating.

**Illnesses Associated with Poor Nutrition**

There are many dangers associated with children developing poor eating habits from an early age. Some of these dangers include actual physical illnesses. Some of these illnesses can have a very negative impact on a child's life in the future. Some of these illnesses can greatly limit the things that they will be able to do. Some of these effects will stop them from being able to live a normal happy life. Some of these effects can be life-threatening and if not controlled can lead to death.

Eating healthy and teaching your children about the benefits of nutritional food is very important and they are never too young to begin teaching them these things. The earlier you teach them the better the effect will be.

The following are some examples of the types of illnesses that can be developed as a result of poor nutrition.

**The Dangers of Poor Nutrition**

Although being over-weight or obese is a serious issue, there are far much worse consequences that can come because of poor nutrition. The scary thing is that some of these illnesses are irreversible. This means that once a person has the illness, they will have it for the rest of their life. I am sure that you do not want your child to have a difficult life and I am positive that you do not want them to have to suffer from an illness for the rest of their life. The best place to start to make sure your child does not develop diet-related illnesses is to make sure that they have healthy eating habits.

The following are some examples of the different types of illnesses that can be developed as a result of poor nutrition:

**Anaemia**

Anaemia is a serious problem, and it can come with a lot of undesired health results. Anaemia is an illness that causes a person's blood to become weak. They have a hard time replacing blood and this leads to some serious problems. Anaemia can cause problems such as shortness of breath. It can also cause dangerous problems such as getting light headed or even fainting when standing. People with anaemia will also have a faster heartbeat and they will feel weak and tired the majority of the time.

**Beriberi**

Beriberi is an illness that affects an individual's ability to turn food into useable energy. This illness is caused by a thiamine deficiency. This disease can cause a person to completely lose their appetite, and this can be very dangerous for your child's health if they stop eating. Beriberi also causes serious problems such as severe weakness. This weakness is even worse in the legs. Those who have Beriberi have a hard time trying to do the simplest things such as standing up.

**Diabetes**

Having a diet that consists of unhealthy food combined with a lack of exercise is a recipe for diabetes. This is especially true for people who have diabetes that already runs in their family. If diabetes is hereditary in your family, you must make sure that your children are eating a nutritional diet. Diabetes is a very serious disease and it can cause some very serious negative health issues. In most cases, diabetes cannot be cured; it can only be managed. I'm sure that you do not want your child to have to be inconvenienced by a life of counting carbs and measuring insulin shots. In severe cases, diabetes can even lead to limbs needing to be amputated as a result of gangrene and even death. There are some more common symptoms of diabetes and the following are a few examples.

Early diabetes will cause a person to always feel thirsty. They will notice that they always feel tired and that they urinate on a more frequent basis. They will often have an appetite that cannot be satisfied and will also experience periods of weight loss. Later more serious symptoms would include periods of blurry vision. They may also experience frequent headaches and periods of dizziness. People with diabetes can develop sores on the bottom of their feet that do not heal, in extreme cases, this can lead to amputation.

After reading all of this information, I am sure that you will do everything you can to make sure that your child has healthy eating habits and that they are getting all the nutrition that they need. As stated earlier in this book, it is your job as a parent to make sure your child is safe and making sure your child is eating right is a form of keeping your child safe.

**Conclusion**

I am sure that just as with all other parents, you want nothing but the best and happiest life for your child or children. One of the best places to start to ensure your child will have a healthy and happy life is to make sure that they are raised with an understanding of how important proper nutrition is.

As stated before, it may be difficult to get your child to eat healthy foods in the beginning. This is especially true when it comes to children that are already used to unhealthy snacks, drinks, and treats. With enough effort and determination, you can surely make it happen though. After all, we are talking about the future of your child so there is no such thing as trying too hard.

You will likely have to try many different types of healthy food before you find the kinds that your child likes. Once you discover healthy food that they do like, make a note of it and then continue trying new things. One trick that is very effective for getting children to eat healthy food is to make it look more appealing by placing it on the plate in creative ways. Make it colourful with healthy dressings.

CHAPTER FOUR

# How To Keep Your Children Healthy

It's perfectly natural for parents to worry about their kids getting sick. Of course, as a mom or dad, you take responsibility for this aspect of your children's health.

Here are some of the most important things you can do to protect your child from diseases:

***Get Your Kids Immunized***

Vaccines are a hot topic these days. But the truth of the matter is that anti-vaccine groups are in the wrong. There are simply too many myths about vaccines being spread by misinformed people or by people who stand to profit because they sell alternative medicines, books, or health programmes.

In other words, believing that vaccines are bad is just as erroneous a belief as believing that Elvis Presley is still alive or that space aliens are living among us. The problem with the anti-vaccine belief is that it puts your children, and other children, at risk.

So get your children immunized, and follow the vaccination schedule recommended by their doctor. The World Health Organization regards vaccines as one of the most effective public health interventions, as it prevents about 2.5 million deaths among children every year. The CDC considers vaccination the 20th century's greatest achievement in public health.

***Have Regular Visits to the Doctor***

This starts early in the life of your child, and it shouldn't stop even as they are in their teens. According to the American Academy of Pediatrics, during your child's first three years, there should be nine checkups at least.

As they grow older, these visits to the doctor need to continue. Of course, some kids may not be all too happy with the idea, so be prepared to set your mind at ease. Kids worry about the pain, the manner of the doctor, or being separated from you. Sometimes it's just the fear of the unknown. You'll need to assuage your kid's feelings of anxiety, although it helps if you choose a kid-friendly clinic where the doctors are experienced or at least skilled in dealing with children. You may not want someone who acts like Dr House in that popular TV show from a few years ago.

You can also reassure your children that all healthy kids get regular checkups. If your child is sick, you can support them by telling them gently about how the sickness isn't their fault and that the doctor can help.

***Get Health Insurance***

Nowadays, getting health insurance is a legal matter now. In most cases, you'll be forced to pay a fine if you don't have your kids insured. But it is also a practical matter. Without adequate health insurance, you may have to foot the medical bills yourself if your child gets sick. That will be far more costly than paying for insurance.

You can start by going to the comprehensive health care website so you can get Medicare or shop for an insurance plan.

These three things cover the very basics of protecting your children from disease. It starts with prevention through immunization, and then with regular visits to the doctor, you can monitor your child's health continuously. With health insurance, you have the means to make sure that your children get the care and medical treatment they require.

## Feed Them Well

When it comes to the health of your children, a large part of it is about making sure they eat the right kinds of food. This isn't always easy. After all, children can be picky about their food and they do tend to make the most unfortunate choices when it comes to snacks.

In their earlier toddler years, you're probably going to rely on your doctor regarding your child's food options, starting with switching from breastfeeding to formula. Then you'll have to deal with baby foods and baby cereals.

When you start feeding him solid food, this is when you need to set the stage for healthier habits for the future. This means introducing vegetables early by giving them options about which vegetables to try out. You can subtly encourage them by eating vegetables yourself while you're with them, instead of forcing them to eat veggies.

In addition, you'll also want to limit your child's exposure to caffeine, sodas, and fast food. This way, they won't be addicted to these unhealthy food items in the future.

***The Basic Rules of Pediatric Nutrition***

The basic rules are simple. Encourage your children to eat a variety of foods. There should be lots of fruits, veggies, and grain products. You also need to make sure that your children have enough iron and calcium to meet the needs of their growing bodies.

Meanwhile, the food items to avoid or limit include dishes that are high in cholesterol, saturated fat, salt, and sugar.

You'll have to accept that some children, especially toddlers, can be very picky eaters. This is normal. All you need to check is that your children are growing heavier and they're developing normally. You can also tell your doctor about your children's food habits so that he can prescribe supplemental vitamins and nutrients that the children's diet isn't providing.

***Recommended Food for Kids***

A lot of kids tend to learn early in life that the so-called "healthy" food items taste much worse than "junk foods" which are regarded as delicious. But there are some healthy food items which are tasty for children.

Examples here include milk, which lots of younger children enjoy. Many older children drink less milk not because they have learned to dislike the taste, but simply because they think that fruit juice and soda are tastier. So by simply limiting these soda and fruit juice drinks, your kids can still enjoy milk more.

For those kids who don't like milk or are intolerant, yoghurt can be a good alternative. Just get a brand that doesn't have extra sugar and is low in fat. If possible, it should contain probiotics, although there is still some debate as to how helpful probiotics are.

Peanut butter is also a rather obvious option. But then again, you should get a brand that's fortified with lots of vitamins. Other healthy options that kids don't usually mind eating include unpeeled apples, eggs every other day, and a serving of tuna every week.

## Introduce Them to Exercises

There was a time when quite a few parents were too concerned about their overly active children, which many believe had given rise to a lot of misdiagnoses of ADHD (attention deficit hyperactivity disorder). But nowadays parents are worrying about inactivity, especially with the popularity of console games, smartphone and tablet video games, the Internet, and of course huge LCD TVs.

***Limiting Inactive Entertainment***

This is probably the first order of business for many parents whose kids stay glued to the TV screen or computer monitor. Limiting a child's exposure to these things can get difficult as kids get older, so it's better if you start early.

The first thing you need to teach children is that watching TV and playing video games are *privileges* that you allow them and not something they are entitled to. So that means you can forbid TVs in kids' bedrooms, disallow TV watching during meals and while doing homework, or even disallow them during weekdays.

The Internet is a different matter, however, because children do need to use them especially for doing their homework. Your best bet is to make sure that your PC is in the living room so that you can monitor their Internet use so can see that they're not viewing inappropriate content.

***Encouraging Exercise***

The next step is getting your kids to get off the couch or bed and become more active. That's not too hard. All you need to do is to *find out* just what kind of activities your kids enjoy.

So for younger children, you can have them play simple tag games, skate, play with a ball, ride a horse, ride a bike, or fly a kite. Many of these things can be taught to kids, such as ball games and riding a bike. You can teach them yourself, or arrange for someone knowledgeable to teach them.

You can also support their desire to play sports. Lots of sports such as baseball have versions for kids. Just don't go overboard and *force* your children to learn. This may cause your kid to rebel and refuse to play anymore. Becoming an overbearing parent who forces their children to excel in sports is not only unbecoming but also counterproductive if your goal is to keep your children healthy through physical activity.

***Safety Precautions***

Of course, getting injuries is going to be part of the deal when you have an active child. This is going to be unavoidable, unfortunately. But you can limit the severity of the injuries by making sure that your children are adequately protected. Many activities and sports mandate that children wear helmets and protective gear. Make sure your child wears them when engaged in sports.

You should also have a first aid kit ready at all times in your car and at home. And finally, don't forget to teach your children some rudimentary first aid measures as well.

## Protect Them from Household Accidents

You may have heard that accidents are the leading cause of death in children. While that's a rather harrowing statistic, at least many of these accidents are preventable. That means you'll need to keep your home (and your car) safe for your kids.

If you have a baby, then your first task is to make sure you get a safe crib. Check that the crib model hasn't been recalled for safety reasons. You should also make sure that it has been assembled correctly.

***Proofing the Home for Younger Children***

For toddlers and preschoolers, you'll need to remember that they can be very active and they can crawl just about anywhere. So that means you need to keep cabinets locked, dangerous stairs blocked, and the pool well-fenced. Make sure there are no dangerous sharp edges and corners on which a child can hit their head.

You'll also need to remember that young children like to put things in their mouths. So this means locking up toxic materials high up where young children can't find them. Other small items which may present a choking hazard must also be collected and kept out of reach.

This may not be enough though, so for very young children constant supervision may be required. In cars, special seats for younger children should be a priority.

***Protecting Older Children***

Just because a child is already older, it doesn't mean they're automatically wiser. So protect them from places and appliances which can hurt them especially when they're alone. Kitchen and ironing appliances are good examples. As children get older, they should be taught show to handle these things safely.

Some households have firearms. While some families advocate educating young children about firearm safety, it is still a good idea that children do not have access to firearms unless they are with a knowledgeable adult. At the very least, guns and rifles should be locked securely so that children couldn't use them when you're not there.

***Alarms and Safety Procedures***

One of the more concrete ways you can make your home safe is by getting the appropriate alarms, so you know when something is wrong. This means installing smoke alarms and carbon monoxide detectors. You may also want to install burglar alarms to supplement your locks.

Then of course you should have a first aid kit available. As an adult, you may want to learn CPR yourself. At the very least, you should have the appropriate emergency phone numbers listed on your mobile phone and near your landline. Aside from the usual 911, you need the number of the local fire department, emergency hospital, and poison control.

Then as your children grow older, they should also learn the basic safety procedures. If you have a fire extinguisher, they should know when and how to use it. They should have a clear plan of action when various alarms (burglar, fire alarm, etc.) go off.

Something always goes wrong, and that's a fact of life. You can prevent many accidents from happening, but preventing them all may not be feasible. Alarms tell you when these things happen, and safety plans and procedures help you know what to do when bad things happen.

## Teach Them Good Habits

Many parents are always worrying about their kids' safety even when they're all grown up. The good news is, you can help protect your kids by teaching them some habits.

We all know about filthy habits like smoking, taking drugs and drinking alcohol which we forbid our children to try. You probably also educate them about avoiding unhealthy habits like drinking soda and eating junk food all the time. But you can also teach them to adopt healthy habits too.

***Hygienic Habits***

Let's start with hygiene since it's a basic aspect of growing up. This means making sure your kids wash up every day, wash their hands before eating, change clothes daily, and refrain from using other people's glasses and utensils.

But one habit that must be taught properly is oral hygiene. Children must learn to brush and floss their teeth properly. While many parents teach these habits, it's still unfortunate that many kids don't know how to brush and floss their teeth. So you need to teach them these things.

***Safety Habits***

These habits include checking both sides of the street before crossing and using a seatbelt. These things should be taught religiously so they become automatic for children even as they grow up.

Then there are the habits that children need to learn when using dangerous tools, such as tools in the garage and appliances in the kitchen. All these things must be shown and practised regularly, and you need to be there when your kids get some hands-on experience.

This extends to healthy habits when driving. Aside from using seatbelts, your children should learn to ignore their phones when they're learning to drive. They should learn to ignore any sort of distraction.

They need to learn to be wary of strangers who talk to them when they're not around. Even people they know can also be dangerous, such as drunken friends behind the wheel of a car. They should also develop the habit of avoiding dangerous items like knives and guns if you're not there with them to supervise then.

***Healthy Nutritional Habits***

One habit you can teach your kids is to incorporate vegetables into their diet. This is the most challenging aspect of teaching proper nutrition. Broccoli and spinach just don't taste as delicious as hotdogs, pizza, and ice cream.

But they can learn to include vegetables if they develop a habit of eating them when they're still young. You can do this by eating veggies with them and making it evident that you like the taste. It's like beer—kids drink them because they see the adults drink them even if the taste isn't exactly like soda. They can learn to view veggies the same way, by learning to enjoy them because you enjoy them too.

Remember, a habit is something you do without thinking, simply because it's the way you learned to do things. By getting a child used to eating veggies and fruits, at least you'll know they'll be healthy when they get older.

CHAPTER FIVE

# Choosing a Childcare Provider

I'm sure that as a parent you are well aware of how expensive it can be to care for your child. Well, guess what, if you are looking for a childcare provider you should prepare yourself for yet another bill, the only difference is that childcare is usually paid weekly.

The following chapter will go over the basics of setting a budget for child care, an average of the costs, as well as some ideas on how you can save money to help with your child care budget.

**Figure Out the Expenses**

As a parent, I am sure that you have already had many headaches in the past that resulted from trying to balance budgets and trying to figure out how to take money from one budget and put it into another. Well, the cold hard truth is that childcare is not cheap, especially if you want your child to be cared for by a reputable provider. One of the smartest things you can do before you even begin looking for a childcare provider is to sit down and figure out exactly what you have to spend each month on child care, or in other words, create a budget. If you create a budget before you begin looking for a child care provider you can avoid being crushed by finding the provider of your dreams and then finding out you cannot afford their services.

The following is a brief guide on how to calculate your child care budget and also some ideas on how to save some money.

**Calculate Income**

The first thing you need to do is find out what everyone's monthly income that will be contributing to the childcare. Add all of these monthly incomes together and you will get the number of the total household income. You want to make sure to include all forms of income and not just primary employment, every dollar counts as budgets are very precise.

**Calculate Expenses**

After you have calculated the monthly income of your household it is time to make a list of all of your expenses for the household and how much each of them is. This list needs to include everything from groceries to the electric bill, to your morning cup of coffee from Starbucks.

**Figure Out What's Left Over**

After you have calculated the monthly income of your household as well as the monthly expenses of your household you need to subtract the expenses from the income. The remaining money will be the money that you will be able to apply to child care without breaking your budget.

In some cases, you may find that there is nothing left over for child care and you are in the hole with your current expenses. If this is the case here are a few examples of things you may need to cut out of your life for a while until you are in a better financial situation.

**Save Whenever You Can**

It is smart as a parent to shop whenever you can when items go on sale. Every little dollar adds up and you will be surprised by how much you can save by buying backpacks or sweaters out of season because they go on sale. Sometimes you can even find them for up to 60% off.

**Adjust Your Spending Habits**

If you are trying to make a budget for child care it is probably not a good idea to be spending money on things that are not necessary. You have to understand that there is a difference between need and want. For example, child care is a need where as a Starbucks mocha latte is a want.

**Buy Used**

You can find some nice clothes and other things at some second-hand stores. Your child grows quite quickly in their early stages and there is no need to be constantly buying them brand-new outfits at expensive retail stores when they will outgrow them in a few months. There is nothing wrong with shopping at second-hand stores and some of them have some very nice things.

You will probably have to make many changes in your life if you want to be able to afford services from a reputable child care provider. Did you know that the average cost of in-home child care is about $650 a month and for day care services it will run you right around $1,000 a month? That is quite a bit of money, isn't it? Do not worry, with proper budgeting and with enough searching you will surely find the child care provider that offers everything your child needs at a price you can afford.

**Get Recommendations**

As a parent who is looking for childcare, you cannot expect that a reputable and trustworthy childcare provider is just going to fall into your lap. You have to think of the process of finding a child care provider kind of like the process of finding a new job. You can't just sit around and hope that one will show up. You have to get out on the grind and find what you are looking for. This process will be made much easier if you get recommendations from reliable sources. This will save you from going from care provider to care provider to only be disappointed.

The following chapter will go over the importance of doing the leg work to find a care provider and will also give you some ideas of where to look for recommendations for reputable child care providers.

**Get Out There!**

Once again, you cannot just sit around and expect the child care provider of your dreams to appear on your doorstep. You will have to do research and acquire recommendations and to be honest with you this process will probably be quite time-consuming. The time and effort will be well worth it though because you surely want the best care possible when it comes to your child.

Recommendations are a great place to start but there are certain things you need to look for before listening to a recommendation. For example, you need to find out if the person who made the recommendation is reliable. You also want to find out if other people have made the same recommendation. After that, you should check to see if the person who made the recommendation had a child that received care from that provider.

It is sad but a fact that some companies pay people to write a review and make recommendations for them. That is why you need to check the credibility of the source of the recommendation. A great place to look for recommendations is from your friends because they will be likely to provide you with honest recommendations. Another great place to look for recommendations is from your co-workers.

Chances are more than a few of your co-workers have at least one child and they surely have someone that looks after them while they are at work. They will surely know a reputable child care provider because just like you, they want nothing but the best for their child. As well, chances are that if you work together, your pay will be similar, which means the chances of you being able to afford the same child care provider are fair.

There are also staffing agencies and other government services which offer reviews on child care providers. The reviews on government websites are much more likely to be reliable than those found randomly on Google.

## Interview Potential Candidates

Once you have done the leg work and have gone through all of the recommendations you will have surely met some potential candidates. You need to interview these candidates and make sure that they fulfil every one of your standards when it comes to the care of your child. Remember you are the parent and you do not have to flex to meet other people's standards.

You are the parent so that makes you in control of this interview process. It is important to remember through this process that some people can be quite deceitful and no matter how sad the truth is, you must keep an eye out for people who are good at hiding their true selves.

**What Should You Ask?**

I cannot express how important it is to interview a childcare provider before you enrol your child in their services. There are some very important questions you should ask during the interview or the tour of the daycare.

These questions will not only ensure the safety of your child but will also help you feel more relaxed about the whole situation as well.

The following are examples of the types of questions you need to ask the childcare provider during your interview.

**What are the Provider's Qualifications?**

You need to ask the childcare provider what their qualifications are. You need to ask them how long they have been in business. As well, you need to get professional references from them. Ask them if they have any reviews they can submit. Find out if they are CPR certified because you never know when an emergency may happen and you want to make sure that the person caring for your child is qualified enough to handle the situation. Another important thing to ask is if the childcare provider is licensed and if they are not I would start looking elsewhere. Another important thing to ask if your child will be going to a daycare centre is if the centre is accredited.

**How Safe is the Center?**

When conducting your interview with your childcare provider you need to ask them how safe their facility is. You need to ask them if electrical sockets are blocked with child protectors and if corners on tables are rounded or covered by child-protectant material. Another important question to ask is if cleaning supplies are locked up. A huge and very important question to ask about safety is what the policy is on people picking up children. You want to make sure that the childcare provider has a strict policy on only approved people picking up the children and also requiring identification. It is advised that you take a tour of the facility to see the safety measures they have taken for yourself. One good idea is while on the tour to look for certification of safety from inspectors because most places will place these on the wall in a visible area.

**What happens if Your Child is Sick?**

You must ask the childcare provider if there is a clear plan in place in the case of a child becoming ill. You need to ask if there are policies on when and if a child will be sent home. It is also important to ask this question because you do not necessarily want your child to spend hours in a place where children can be sick and not be sent home. The last thing you want is for your child to be perfectly healthy and then come home sick. Another important question to ask is if you will be charged for the days that you have to keep your child at home because they are too ill to go to daycare.

**What is the Ratio When Comes to Children and Staff**

If you are choosing to enrol your child in a daycare facility rather than home care you must ask the provider what the staff-to-child ratio is. You do not want your child to be in a place where they will be lost in the crowd. You typically want to try and find a childcare provider that can offer smaller room sizes and fewer children per staff. This will ensure that your child is still receiving attention and that all of their needs are being met. Keep in mind, a child needs a lot of attention and needs to feel like they matter.

**What is the Parenting Style and What Curriculum is used?**

You must ask the childcare provider what type of curriculum will be taught and what form of parenting will be used. You need to find out if there will be structure and what type of methods will be used to redirect your child's negative behaviour.

**Do They Offer Transportation?**

Some childcare providers offer transportation if it is needed, and this can be a great convenience for some people. Make sure you ask if transportation is available.

**What is the Visitation Policy?**

Plain and simple, stay away from childcare providers who require prior notice to you coming to see your child. It is your child after all and you should be able to visit them whenever you please. Childcare providers who require prior notice to visitation usually have something to hide and that is why they want to know when you are going to come. You want to try and find a place that has an open-door policy for the parent. Better yet, you want to try and find a childcare provider that not only allows you to drop by unexpectedly but encourages it. Parent participation in childcare services and crucial so the parents should be there visiting as much as possible.

The process of trying to find childcare services that fulfil your every desire can be quite time-consuming and seem hopeless at times. As long as you keep searching and keep questions like the ones listed above in your mind you will surely be successful with your efforts. Just remember, no matter how hard it may be, it is important that you find the best care possible for your child as you will trust this person with your child.

You will probably have some of your questions that you would like to ask as well and that is good. There is nothing wrong with asking the child care provider every question that comes to your mind. If they are a good child care provider they will understand all of your questions and will appreciate the fact that you care about your child. The child care providers that seem annoyed with your questions are the ones that you want to avoid.

**Do a Background Check**

Today, you cannot put your trust in a stranger. No matter how much a person may seem as if you can trust them or seem as if they are a good person, you have to be cautious with the amount of trust you put into them.

When it comes to your child and the care that they receive I am positive that you want to ensure that they are in safe hands. Many people in the world are very deceitful and may seem like good people but, are not. There are also many people out there who do some very bad things and that is why you must ensure that the person taking care of your child is good.

If you are not sure of how to check to see if a person has been truthful about who they are the following chapter is perfect for you. In this chapter, we will go over background checks and how you can have one done on someone or a facility.

**Check the Facts**

Many people have mastered the art of deception. They can easily fool other people and manipulate them into believing whatever they want them to. This is true even for those who offer childcare. You must check the facts on your childcare provider and do a background check on them.

There are many different ways you can do a background check on a person. One way is the countless companies that advertise background checks on the internet. These companies will give you all the information they can find about someone for a monthly or yearly fee. It will show all of their criminal histories which can be a vital tool when trying to select a childcare provider. Some of these online background checks can be quite costly however and even if you are just trying to look up the facts in person they will still charge you the entire subscription price. It is important to get your background check done by a company with a good reputation. You need to be sure that they will dig deep and offer you accurate and detailed information on the person you are doing the check on.

You can also perform a background check on your own. It will require much more time and effort than hiring an agency to do it but it is possible. If you do it on your own you will have to do a lot of research on the internet as well as BBB. It would also be a good idea to go to your local courthouses and ask if there is a public file on the person. Doing the check on your own is possible and will save money but in the long run, it is better to use an agency to do the digging for you. They will be much more likely to find something buried if it exists than you will be.

After you have performed this background check as well as all the previous steps it is time to come up with a decision. You need to weigh out all of your desires with your possible candidates. You will know which one is right for you based on how they meet all of your requirements. All of your hard work will finally pay off and you will have the perfect child care provider for you and your child.

**Your Child's Actions and Behaviours**

When you are using the services of a child care provider it is extremely important and necessary for you to monitor the behaviour of your child once they are no longer around the provider.

The sad truth is that there are people out there who will not treat your child with the best of intentions. I know we have all seen the TV shows or have seen it on the news when a child has been mistreated by a child care provider. That is why it is so important for you to monitor the behaviour of your child at home to make sure they are being treated correctly and that they are happy with their childcare provider.

The following chapter will discuss some of the common signs that a child is being mistreated while under the care of a child care provider. Pay close attention and retain this information as it is extremely important.

**What to Watch For**

There are some signs that you need to watch for when you are using the services of a childcare provider. These signs are important to look for because if they are exhibited, something is wrong, and the better the child is removed from the setting the better.

The following are some signs that you should watch out for when using a daycare or home child care provider.

**Is Your Child Afraid?**

Does your child seem afraid of the daycare or child care provider? Do they scream or throw a fit every time you take them to the facility? This is a common sign of a child being abused or neglected at a daycare and it should raise serious concerns.

**Is Your Child Becoming Dethatched?**

Does it seem as if your child is becoming socially detached from the world? Is your child beginning to isolate themselves? This is also another sign to look out for because children who are being mistreated will begin to shut themselves off from society to protect themselves.

**Is Your Child Becoming Less Interested?**

If you notice that your child begins to lose interest in things that once entertained them there may be something going on with your child care provider. A common sign of child abuse or neglect is a child becoming uninterested in things in life and becoming cold in a sort of way.

**Is Your Child Happy?**

The most obvious sign of something going on with your child care provider is if your child begins to show signs of being unhappy. This sign does not even necessarily mean that there is abuse going on, the child might just not like the environment of the daycare or the child care provider. In either case, it is time to find another option for your child because you must do everything you can to ensure that they are happy and content, always!

In summary, finding a childcare provider that suits all of your needs and desires can be quite difficult and can consume a large amount of time. All the effort and time are well worth it though when you think about the safety and happiness of your child.

Just remember all of the things that were discussed in this book and all of the valuable information you retained. This information will surely be helpful if you apply it to your search for a perfect child care provider. Keep in mind, you may not find the perfect fit the first time around. It may be a trial and error thing where you have to try several providers before you find the correct fit. Just do no give up hope and keep trying because you will surely find the child care provider of your dreams, sooner or later.

It is understandable if you experience anxiety when you think of trusting your child with a stranger but what are you going to do, take your child to work with you every day? Surely not! You have to let go of that anxiety and relax a little. All you need to do is follow the steps that were listed in this book and your child will be just fine.

I hope this book has been helpful for you and has made it a little bit easier for you to make a selection on your child care provider. I wish you the best of luck and I thank you for your time!

CHAPTER SIX

# Creating Childhood Confidence

Confidence is extremely important for a child to develop in the early stages of their life. It is important because it is needed to overcome many obstacles that your child will face in life. It is the job of the parent of the child to help the child build self-confidence. There are many ways that you can help your child build confidence.

Building your child's self-confidence will not only make them feel good about themselves but also prepare them for the future as well. You may find yourself asking: What can I do to give my child higher self-confidence? The answer is not difficult and there are several things you can do daily that will help and they will only take a few minutes.

The following chapters will provide you with some helpful information on the importance of building self-confidence and ways in which to do so. Make sure to pay close attention and take in all the information and building your child's confidence will be a much easier task.

If you are new to parenting, there are probably many things that you are not completely sure of how to do. One of these things may be how important building confidence in your child is or how to build confidence. Do not worry;

just as with every other challenge you have faced in life, it is achievable. All you need to do is learn some helpful techniques and set aside some extra time for your child and building their self-confidence will be as easy as a walk in the park.

A person's confidence levels as an adult are greatly impacted by the level of confidence that they had as a child. This is one of the main reasons why it is so important that you instil a healthy amount of confidence into your child. With a little bit of effort and time, your child will surely develop this crucial life skill.

There are a few things that as a parent you will need to do. The following are some examples:

**Always Make Time**

You must always make time for your child, no matter how busy you are! Showing that your child comes before everything else is an excellent way of building a child's self-confidence and self-worth. It is advisable to take the time to schedule activities with your child that can help with the process of building their confidence. This could be taking them to do something they are good at or maybe even taking them to try something new. This will show them that they are talented which is a great confidence booster. One example could be taking a child to the park for a game of ball. If your child is not into sports, take them to an event that will allow them to show their knowledge of things and always be sure to show how impressed you are.

**Don't Be Too Hard**

Although it is important not to be too easy on your child, it is also important not to be too tough on your child as well. Being too easy on your child will likely not instil proper morals in a child or teach them to be responsible. On the other hand, being too tough will likely lead to low self-confidence because a child will feel as if they never do anything right. You as a parent must find the middle ground and be equal with your discipline. Not every child will respond to the same type of parenting so it is important to experiment and see what works best when it comes to building your child's confidence.

**Be a Positive Example**

It is your job as a parent to set a positive example for your child and to be a role model. One of the personality traits that your child will likely learn from you is your level of self-confidence. You must always appear as if you have a situation under control and that you completely believe in yourself. Also, never talk negatively about yourself in front of your child because this will likely cause them to develop the same habit.

**Watch Out for Bullies**

Bullying is becoming increasingly popular. This is likely stemming from the fact that kids can bully one another at any time and any place, thanks to social media. Bullying is probably one of the quickest ways a child's self-confidence can be destroyed. Bullies often suffer from low confidence in themselves. And to try to make themselves feel better, they try to lower others' confidence as well. This is why you must watch out for the signs of your child being bullied and put an immediate end to it! A few examples of behaviours your child may exhibit while being bullied are:

- Suddenly no longer wants to go to school
- Depression
- Anxiety
- Fear
- Less Social Interactions
- Not seeming Like Themselves

- Not Wanting to Talk About Their School Day

If you notice any of these signs you need to take immediate action!

## Believe In Your Child

You must believe in your child. This is a very simple task to do and requires little effort. However, it is still very important. There are many different ways that you can let your child know you believe in them. With enough effort and time, you will be able to find activities that greatly improve your child's confidence while showing that you believe in them.

Many people may be unsure of how to perform this step effectively and may not have an idea of where to begin. Are you one of these people? If the answer is yes, do not worry, children do not come with guidebooks but you can get advice from places such as this book.

**Show That You Believe in Them**

The process of showing your child that you believe in them can be completed in many different ways. Often, what works for one child may not have the same impact on another. This means that you will likely have to try different things until you find something that works. If you do not know where to start, a few examples are provided below:

**Encourage Your Child to Try New Things**

Encouraging your child to try new things is an excellent way of building their confidence and showing them that you fully believe in their abilities to accomplish something.

Pay attention to the things that your child tells you, especially when it comes to what they would like to do but do not feel that they would be any good at it. Use this situation as a way to show you believe in them by encouraging them to try. Tell them that you believe in them and that they can do anything they set their mind to. It is important to explain to them that they may not be great at something when they first start but over time and with practice they will get much better.

**Push Them Out of Their Comfort Zone**

When a child is stuck in a comfort zone, their chances of building their self-confidence are much slimmer than that of a child who is always challenging themselves. Teaching your child to challenge themselves will greatly improve their self-confidence while at the same time showing them that you believe that they can do anything.

**Brag about Your Child**

Bragging about your child can be a great way to build their confidence and show them that you believe in them. This is especially true if the bragging is done in front of them. Tell other people about their accomplishments and the things you think they will achieve in future as this will surely boost their confidence. Do not brag too much though because this may cause the child to become big-headed.

**Achievements and Fears**

Acknowledging your child's fears, as well as their achievements, is vital in the role of helping your child develop a healthy level of self-confidence. This is especially true when a child triumphs over their fear to accomplish something. It is important to remember that while trying to build a child's confidence, every little accomplishment should be noted. No matter how small the task is, your child will greatly benefit from your acknowledging their accomplishment.

The following paragraphs will give you some helpful information that can assist you with acknowledging your child's achievements and fears. It will serve as your guide so pay careful attention and make sure to retain all the information as it will surely help your child in becoming a self-confident person.

**Praise Their Achievements, Understand Their Fears**

A parent's role in praising their child's achievements as well as understanding their fears are two topics that we will go over in this chapter. Parents need to understand that both are equally important when it comes to the process of instilling confidence in their children. We will go over the importance of and the ways to praise a child's achievements first.

**Praise Their Achievements**

Praising your child's achievements, no matter how small they may seem to you, is vital in the process of creating confidence. This will make your child feel good about themselves and will also create self-confidence because they will feel as if they are constantly doing things that impress you.

Praising your child's achievements can have more of a positive outcome than constantly pointing out the negative things your child might do. This is not surprising since always pointing out the wrong thing a child does makes them feel as if they cannot do anything right. On the other hand, always praising your child's achievements and not talking to them about mistakes that they are making will have negative outcomes as well. This is because the child will feel as if they can do nothing wrong. It is important to find a healthy balance between pointing out mistakes and praising achievements.

When praising your child's achievements, you must be careful to spoil or over-treat them. If you provide your child with a large reward every time they complete a small task, they will naturally begin to think that this will happen every time they do something. This can lead to negative behaviours when the rewards stop as the child will be confused about why they no longer receive a reward for a certain task. It is advised that rewards be saved for bigger accomplishments. When it comes to smaller achievements, verbal recognition or a pat on the back will suffice just fine.

**Understand Your Child's Fears**

Understanding your child's fears also play a big role in the development of your child's self-confidence. You may be asking: "How can fear make my child more confident in himself?" The answer is the fact that overcoming fear can boost a person's self-confidence dramatically. While trying to overcome fears, it is important that you first understand them.

You do not want to set your child up for failure. Some of the things they may be scared to attempt may be too difficult for them. One of the worst things you can do while trying to build a child's confidence is to put them in a situation where they will not win. You need to talk to your child and discover what it is that they are afraid of attempting and determine if it would be a good idea to push your child toward facing those fears.

Once you understand your child's fears and have determined the possible negative and positive outcomes of facing them, you may decide to motivate your child to face those fears. Accomplishing a task that a child once feared they would fail is probably one of the best ways to build their self-confidence. This is because this process shows them that they can do things, no matter how hard they are or scared they were if they just put their mind to it.

It is important to not push your child into facing too many of their fears. Pushing your child too hard may result in an outcome completely different from the one you desire. It may make the child anxious which could have an impact on the rest of their life. This makes further lowers their self-confidence because the anxiety may keep them from being able to accomplish other tasks that they could do effortlessly at one point.

**Teach Them to Learn from Errors**

There is no perfect person in the world. Everyone makes mistakes. The important thing is that we learn to develop ourselves and learn lessons from our mistakes. We must then use these lessons to keep us from making future mistakes of a similar type. It is all part of the growing process. It is the same for a child who needs to build self-confidence.

**Help Them Learn**

Your child has been in the world for much less time than you have. Therefore, it only makes sense that the responsibility of teaching your child how to learn from mistakes falls upon you. As a parent, you have surely had to do this many times in the past and have much more experience with it than your child. As stated before, everyone makes mistakes and no one is perfect. What divides people into those who succeed and those who don't is whether a person learns from their mistakes or not.

Building your child's self-confidence is possible through success, and success is possible through your child learning from their mistakes. You must teach your child not to be too hard on themselves or beat themselves up when they make a mistake. You must teach them to look at the situation from a logical standpoint and determine the things that they could have done differently to get a more desirable outcome. You will be surprised at how much this will boost your child's self-confidence. This process will mature your child's thinking process and they will be more confident because they will know that even if they do not succeed at something the first time, they will determine their mistakes, try again and succeed.

Not teaching your child about learning from their mistakes will eventually have negative outcomes on your child's self-confidence. If your child does not learn from their mistakes, they or will likely keep making the same mistakes. This can make a child feel as if they are stuck in a rut or like success is hopeless. They will feel like they cannot do anything and their motivation toward life will slowly spiral downward. A perfect example of this would be most people in correctional institutions, whether adult or juvenile.

If you ask most of the people in there, they will likely say that they never had anyone teach them the value of learning from their mistakes. These people continued to make the same mistakes until they felt as if life was hopeless and completely gave up on trying to be successful. You do not want this to happen to your child. For you to avoid a situation like this, you must teach your child the importance of learning from their mistakes.

**Accept Who Your Child Is**

Accepting a child for who they are is usually not a difficult task for a parent to perform. On the other hand, there are instances where certain things about a child bother their parents. This can be extremely damaging to a child's self-confidence because their parents are supposed to be a source of continued approval and affection. There are certain things that a child may not be able to change about themselves and you will have to accept them if you ever want your child to be happy and have high levels of self-confidence.

The following paragraphs will provide you with some examples of types of things some parents may have to learn to accept. Keep in mind, some of these things may be difficult to accept or may even go against your religious background, but if you want your child to be confident and succeed you must accept them.

**Accept Your Child for Who They Are**

There may be certain things about your child that you wish could be different. The truth is, your child cannot change certain things about themselves. You cannot blame your child for who they are, they did not ask to be brought into the world, and you decided to give them life. Your child may also do certain things in their life that you do not approve of but you must accept them as reality and figure out a way to help your child change the behaviours.

The following are some examples of types of things your child cannot change about themselves.

**Sexuality**

This is probably the area where most parents have a hard time accepting their children for who they are. This may be due to moral standpoints or it may be due to religious backgrounds and personal beliefs. No matter what the reason is, you must learn to accept your child for who they are. Showing your child that you love them for who they are will greatly improve their self-confidence and make them feel much better about themselves. Apart from this, trying to force your child to change something about themselves such as sexuality will cause many difficulties for a child in life. They will most likely become confused about who they truly are and this will surely destroy their future and confidence.

**Likes and Dislikes**

You have to learn to accept your child's likes, dislikes, and interests. You have to understand that just because you want your son to grow up to be a football player or your daughter to be a beauty queen does not mean they want the same for their life. You need to encourage your child to do the things they like in life, even if they do not adhere to your set dreams and goals of your child. After all, it is their life, and they are the ones who have to live it; parents are just passengers on the journey used as guidance.

**Accept Your Child's Strengths and Weaknesses**

It is important for you as a parent to understand that it may not be possible for your child to live up to all of your expectations. You must remember to be realistic with your expectations for your child and to be understanding when they cannot live up to one of them. If you constantly show disapproval when a child cannot meet one of your expectations, you will destroy the child's confidence and make them feel like a lesser person or worthless. Showing your child that you will accept them as long as they try their best in everything, they do will surely boost their confidence and make them happier people with a more successful life.

These were just a few examples of the countless things you may have to accept about your child one day. As stated before, you do not have to like everything your child does, but you must learn how to accept it, not only for the confidence and well-being of the child but also for your own as well.

**Take Interest in Your Child's Life**

While your child is growing, you need to be actively involved in their life and provide opportunities for growth if you want them to be full of confidence and success. Spending time with your child is really all that this step requires. Do some activities with your child that they enjoy and use this time to learn more about your child's life. The more you know about what is going on in your child's life the better you will be able to help them in building their confidence.

Here are some helpful hints for being involved in your child's life and opening up opportunities for them.

**Be Involved**

It is important that as a parent you make sure to be involved in your child's life. This does not mean when it is convenient for you, it means at all times, even when difficult. You may have to do things you are not interested in or attend events that you may find boring. It does not matter, you need to be involved. Being involved in your child's life shows them that you truly care for them and at the same time build their self-worth and self-confidence.

You need to ask your child questions about their life and about how they feel everything is going for them. You need to try to figure out the areas where you can help them to build their confidence and open new opportunities for them during these discussions. A great time to do this would be during dinner, with the family eating as a whole at the dining table and not in front of the TV on the couch.

While it is important to get out and do things that your child is interested in while trying to be more involved with their life, you need to set specific family times that the entire family spends time as a whole. This greatly nurtures the health of a family relationship and makes your child more likely to open up to you about their life. If your child is open with you, they will tell you what is holding their confidence back which allows you to help them gain their confidence back and be successful.

You need to take extra care not to pry into your child's life too deeply. Trying to be too involved in your child's life might make your child feel as if you are invading their life or trying to control it. You must keep in mind that it is their life and although you may not agree with some of their decisions, you have to let them learn on their own. Having a healthy amount of involvement without trying to invade your child's life is the perfect recipe for a happy family and a confident child.

Provide Responsibilities

Responsibilities in life are very important for a child, especially when it comes to building their confidence. You must be realistic with the responsibilities you set for your child because you do not want to doom them to failure. Setting responsibilities that are too difficult may fail which will further lower your child's confidence. On the other hand, a child who performs their responsibilities correctly will be granted better self-confidence.

The following are some ideas on where to start when it comes to setting responsibilities for your child.

**Set Responsibilities, Be Realistic**

While setting responsibilities for your child, it is important that you set realistic responsibilities. It is advised that you start with simple responsibilities and work toward the larger ones, once the smaller ones can be executed with minimal effort.

The ideal basic responsibilities to start with for children would be tasks such as cleaning their room and making their bed. After they can handle this daily, you may want to begin adding additional responsibilities such as doing the dishes a few times a week or vacuuming the carpet.

As a child gets older and can handle more responsibilities, it is time to make their responsibilities more difficult. One idea that may be suitable is getting your child a pet. Something smaller than a dog is advised because most people do not realize how much care a dog needs. It may be better to start with an animal such as a hamster or some fish. The act of having to feed this animal daily, while taking care of its other needs, will help your child to become more responsible. Properly completing their responsibilities will also create more self-confidence for them since they will see they can do challenging things.

Instilling responsibilities into your child's daily life will be a challenge at first, but with determination and effort, it will be effective in boosting your child's confidence.

**Poor Self Confidence**

A child with poor self-confidence will almost certainly have a much more challenging life than a confident child. Having good confidence causes a person to have certain traits in their character while having low self-confidence creates negative traits in people's characters.

The following are a few examples of the countless disadvantages that low confidence can have on your child's life.

**The Dangers of Low Self-Confidence**

Many different disadvantages come with having low confidence levels. These disadvantages can have a huge negative impact on a person's current life as well as their future. That is why it is so important to instil high levels of confidence into your child, even from a very early age.

Some examples of the negative impacts low self-confidence can have on a child are as follow:

**Scared to Try New Things**

If your child has low levels of self-confidence, they will likely find it difficult to try new things. The fear of failure will take them over, time and time again. This fear will stop them dead in their tracks every time they think of trying to do something new.

**Bad Social Impacts**

If your child suffers from low self-confidence, they will likely experience difficulty with their social life in the future. A task as simple as approaching someone to say hello can feel impossible if a person has low self-confidence.

To be able to speak to other people and keep your head high, you must have good self-confidence. This can also extend into the classroom and your child's learning. For example, if your child has very low levels of confidence, they will likely be afraid of approaching a teacher and asking for help with what they don't understand. They would rather just take a failing grade because they do not have to interact socially in this way.

**Emotional Issues**

Certain emotional problems will likely be caused by long periods of low confidence. These emotional problems may include loss of happiness, anxiety, depression, irritability, and in extreme cases, suicide. Suicide most often occurs when a child feels as if they are nothing and will never be anything. Sometimes they hide this feeling from their parents and other times their parents do not pay enough attention, either way, it is terrible that a child would do this.

All these emotional issues can have impacts on your child's present and future life. That is why it should be your top priority as the parent of your child to ensure that they feel great about themselves and that they have high levels of self-confidence.

Just keep in mind all the negative consequences that were discussed in this chapter while remembering that there are countless more and you will surely be motivated to start helping your child to better their confidence.

In conclusion, your child might be currently suffering from low levels of self-worth and self-confidence, but it does not have to be that way forever. You as a parent must take the necessary steps that will ensure that your child has a bright future full of potential and opportunities. The first place to start with this is to make sure your child feels good about themselves and has healthy levels of self-worth and self-confidence because these are two traits that make life's challenges bearable and possible of overcoming.

Without the building block of confidence, your child will likely be lost once it comes time for them to experience the real world. Without the capability of approaching unfamiliar people or taking on new tasks, the simplest tasks in life can be made a hundred times more difficult. Confidence is more than just an admired trait. To be truly successful in life and to be happy with themselves, your child must learn to be confident.

While motivating your child to build their self-confidence, remember the tips and tricks as well as the advice you have received from this book as it will be a valuable guide to assist you through the process. As well, make sure to keep in mind the negative outcomes that can become reality if your child doesn't have a healthy level of confidence.

**Teaching Children About Money**

Children grow up to be adults. The lessons they learn as children will be carried with them as they become students, employees, husbands and wives, parents, and grandparents.

If they learn the lessons when they're younger, the mistakes in adulthood are less frequent and less disastrous.

Some of those lessons learned in childhood relate to love, work, and values. You teach your child the things that are important to you and the lessons you want them to learn to be successful, happy, and productive. Unfortunately, one lesson that's often neglected is the lesson of money. Whether it's because parents don't feel confident talking about money or they don't think it is important, many children grow up without money skills.

This isn't a lesson that you want to learn when you're an adult. The consequences are too significant. They include financial stress, which can cause illness. Other consequences are debt, no savings, living paycheck to paycheck, and a life that's more difficult than it needs to be. As a parent, there is a responsibility to teach your child to be money smart.

**What does it mean to be money smart?**

There are different components of being money smart. They include the concept of saving, goal setting, and making your money work for you. Money smart means knowing that instant gratification isn't always as satisfying as it might be, and saving for something you want can pay off in ways that you just cannot imagine.

**Teaching your child to be money-smart means teaching them:**

- About saving money
- About the importance of financial goals (long-term and short-term)
- How to invest their money and make their money work for them

- How to budget and allocate their money so they can pay for what they need and want
- How to leverage technology and systems to stay in control of their money
- That they're the only person who can make decisions about their money
- About the practice of giving or donating to help others in need
- How to decide if they are going to spend money now or save it for later
- How banks work
- How to earn money and achieve their financial goals

These are some heavy lessons and, in many cases, they're lessons that need to be learned over time. However, when you spend the time and energy teaching your child to be money smart, they will grow up to be confident with their money. You can trust that they'll be able to go out into the world and stay out of financial trouble.

How often do you feel stressed about money? Whether you're trying to pay bills, save for your child's college or your retirement, money stress is a common problem amongst American households. There are probably steps you wish you'd taken and mistakes you wish you hadn't made. And there is a good chance that you also hope that your child has it easier.

There are many reasons why teaching your child about money is so important.

- You want them to be less stressed about their finances when they're adults.

- You want them to be able to live comfortably.
- You don't want them living at home when they're adults because they cannot afford to live on their own.
- You want them to do better than you.
- Bankruptcies and Debt

Learning about money now can help your child avoid some of the biggest money mistakes that people make. Perhaps you've made these mistakes yourself. We're talking about deep debt and bankruptcy. Here are a few statistics to consider:

Every year, more than two million people in America file for bankruptcy. The average American household with at least one credit card has nearly $15,950 in credit card debt (in 2012), according to CreditCards.com.

According to the Department of Education, the default rate on federal student loans has risen by about 5% in the past year and 500,000 more borrowers have slipped into default.

Teaching your child about money and starting when they're young can help them avoid these unfortunate situations. No one wants financial stress and presumably, no one wants to file for bankruptcy or go into massive debt.

It happens from poor planning, overspending, and not knowing how to save for the future. These are the lessons you can teach your child now. It doesn't matter if they're six or sixteen; it's never too early or too late to start. That brings us to the next topic to look at - when can you start teaching your child about money and how do you go about it?

## When to Teach Your Child about Money

You might be surprised to learn that you can start teaching your child about money when they're two years old. While your child may be older than that right now, it's important to get started teaching them about money as soon as possible. And it's never too late to begin.

Let's look at the concepts that you can teach your child at every age.

**Preschool**

At this age, you can teach your child about the concept of money - in other words, what money is and what it is not. You can talk to them about the value of different coins and bills. You can also teach them that money is used to buy things. Playing a store is an easy way to begin teaching the concept of money to young children.

**Early Elementary School**

At this age, it's a great time to start teaching about the difference between a want and a need. Children can help with grocery shopping and begin to participate in decision-making. This is also a great age to begin showing your child how to use a piggy bank and to introduce the concept of an allowance and working for money. By the end of elementary school, they should understand saving money to buy things that they want.

**Junior High School**

At this age, children are more than ready to begin earning money. You can tie allowance to chores or give them opportunities to earn money around the home. It's also a good time to teach them about saving for their future and for things that they want to buy soon. At this age, a child can also begin to learn about investing and leveraging their money.

**High School**

By this time, your child should have learned some financial independence. Hopefully, they've had the opportunity to work for money and have learned about saving for both short-term and longer-term goals. They may have an investment account and be actively saving money for college.

Once your child is in college they will be well on their way to financial independence. Sure, you may be paying for college and helping them manage their finances. However, they should also be able to handle most of their financial decisions on their own.

It's never too late to begin teaching your child about money, saving, and investing. Next, we'll talk about opportunities to teach your child about money. Teachable moments happen often; the trick is learning to recognize them.

## When to Talk to Your Child about Money

Teaching your child about money takes more than one conversation. Using real-life situations and examples will help them pull the concepts together. They'll learn not only from your words but also through your actions. Here are a few ideas and opportunities to talk to your child about money.

**When They Receive Monetary Gifts**

When your child receives a gift for their birthday or another holiday, it's a great time to talk to them about saving some of the money. You can even help them plan how they're going to save and what to save for.

**When You Visit the ATM**

The ATM is a magic box that spits out money when you enter a secret code. If only! But that's what children might think if you don't talk to them about what the ATM is and how it works. It's a great opportunity to talk about earning, saving, and making spending decisions.

**When You are Shopping**

Chances are that your child goes with you when you head to the supermarket and run other errands. This is an ideal opportunity to explain to your child about budgeting. You can also talk about how different items cost different amounts. You can even ask your child to help you compare prices and find the cheapest-priced item.

**Paying Bills**

Paying bills is probably not something that you usually do with your child. However, it's a great time to talk to your child about what some of the things that they take for granted cost. You can talk about working and responsibilities and how you pay for these expenses each month.

It's also a good opportunity to talk to your child about different ways to save money and why you might want to save money. For example, you can talk about turning the lights off when they leave a room and using any energy savings to put toward something fun for the family like a vacation.

**Creating Your Monthly Budget**

Many adults intentionally don't talk about money in front of their children. However, in many cases, that's a mistake. When children are aware of the family finances and understand income and expenses, it helps them envisage the big picture. Of course, you don't want to create added stress for your child if there are financial difficulties. However, involving them in discussions about your budget helps them have a better understanding of money.

**Allowance Time**

If you give your child an allowance, it's an opportunity to talk about their decisions and what they're going to do with the money. Depending on your child's age you may have requirements for their allowance. For example, you may require them to donate some and save some as well.

With busy lives, it's easy to overlook opportunities to teach your child about money. However, they're present almost every day. Take advantage of them from time to time and involve your child in your financial decisions and responsibilities to help them learn, both through words and actions, about money.

In addition to times and opportunities to teach your child about money, there are also simple tools you can use. They range from a basic piggy bank to mobile applications.

## Tools to Teach Children about Money

Parents can talk and talk about money and children will only retain part of what you say. To back up the important lessons and conversations you want to teach your child through your actions. It's also often useful if the information is experienced or comes from another source. The following tools will help you teach your child about money.

**Piggy bank** – The piggy bank is likely a child's first introduction to saving money. However, simply plunking pennies into the bank doesn't accomplish much. Consider helping your child set a savings goal. For example, maybe they can save for a trip to the toy store.

**Allowance** – If you choose to give your child an allowance, this is the perfect opportunity to teach about saving, spending, and donating. You can require your child to work for their allowance, give them a predetermined amount of money each week or month (which teaches them to budget their money) or a combination of both.

**Books** – There are many books for young children. One book, titled Money Mama & The Three Little Pigs by Lori Mackey, teaches the basics of money and has a positive approach.

**Videos** – Young children love to watch videos and Sesame Street has "For Me, For You, For Later," a fun video about saving, donating, and spending money.

**Games** – Finally, you can find great online games, mobile applications and websites dedicated to teaching kids about money. Buy it Right is a board game by Learning Resources that takes players on a shopping trip and helps them learn about saving money.

Games, books, and other tools help you reinforce the message that you want to teach your child about money. They make it possible to introduce the topic of money to even very young children. Of course, children also spend a good amount of time watching what you do and how you manage your money. Next, we'll talk about teaching your child about budgeting.

## Teach Your Child about Budgeting

Budgeting is something that most adults struggle with. And it's a simple tool that reliably helps you control your money (instead of the other way around). If you can teach your child not only about the concept of budgeting but help them embrace the practice at a young age, they may spend their entire adult lives feeling financially stable and in control of their money.

Imagine what a great gift that is to a child. So how can you teach a child about budgeting? There are a few steps that you can take, and they begin at home.

**Talk about Your Household Budget**

The very first step to teaching your child about the concept of a budget is to involve them in discussions about your budget. Children pay attention to the actions of the people around them. It's ineffective to talk about a budget but not keep one yourself. So, if you don't create a monthly budget, now is the time to be a good example. And if you do, great. Now is the time to involve your child in the budget discussions. Show them your budget. Talk about how much you make and how much goes to the various expenses that they might take for granted, like utilities and food. Also, show them the savings column in your budget so that they know you practice what you preach.

Talk about what you do when you have an excess each month and what you do when you spend more than you've budgeted. Make the family budget a family conversation. Your child will not only learn good budgeting habits themselves, but they'll also have a better understanding of your family finances.

**Give Them Money and Take Them Shopping**

The next step to teach your child about budgeting is to give them money and take them shopping. There are many ways that you can approach this. However, you must be prepared to manage the consequences.

For example, if you give your junior high school child $200 to go school shopping there is a very good chance they're going to mess up and buy one shirt and one pair of pants. The money is gone and now your child is left wearing the same shirt and pants for the school year. Money lessons are often learned by making mistakes.

Be sure that you are willing to follow through on the consequences. If you go out and buy your child more clothing, they don't learn the lesson about budgeting their money and trying to purchase less expensive items so their money stretches further.

You can make it a game at the supermarket, too. Give them $20 for example and ask them to find the items on a list and to stay within the budget. These small experiences help your child begin to realize that they have control over their financial decisions and that there are consequences to spending more than they have.

**Help Them Create a Budget**

When your child is old enough and perhaps has some money coming in, you can help them create a budget for themselves. The budget might contain expenses like gas for the car, money for going out with friends, and a clothing budget. Creating the budget and sticking to it are two different things. Help your child create a plan to stick to their budget. It might require them to keep their receipts or only take out a certain amount of cash each week.

Budgeting is a skill. The earlier your child begins learning and practising this skill, the better. They'll be able to go out into the world confident that they are fully capable of managing their finances. Of course, they may make some mistakes along the way. You've likely made a few of your own. These mistakes are teachable moments.

## Your Child's Money Mistakes

Money mistakes happen. You think you're going to have enough, and you don't. You spend more than you have and then must go without. You get into debt and then must scrimp and struggle to pay it off. Money mistakes aren't fun.

As adults, the consequences of making money mistakes can be high. Children make money mistakes, too. The repercussions may be painful for them; however, they're also valuable teachable moments. Here are some of the mistakes a child might make and some ideas on how to leverage them.

They save for a toy or item that they want and then have buyer's remorse. Buyer's remorse is a bummer. When your child experiences this money mistake there are a few things you can do to help them avoid this mistake in the future.

You can motivate them to always make sure they want an item before they buy it. They can ask themselves a few questions like, "Why do I want this item?" "What do I expect this purchase to do for me?" "Is there a better way to spend my money?" You can also help them return the item. They may not get their full money back, but they'll learn to ask for more from the items they purchase.

They blow their allowance right away and don't have any money to go out with their friends. Don't bail them out. Don't give them opportunities to earn extra money and don't let them borrow money (this teaches them that it's okay to go into debt). Let them miss the outing with friends. They'll be better at budgeting their money the next month.

They spend their entire budget on one brand-name item. This happens to most children. They have money to spend, maybe from a birthday check, and they head to the store and blow it all on one item. Many children feel a bit sad when they get home and realize they only have one thing to show for their money. It's great if you can stop them before they head to the cash register.

Point out a few items that they might like that cost less than the single item they're buying. For example, you're at a clothing store with your tween. They have picked an expensive sweater that they love. You point out that they can get three shirts for the price of that sweater and they'll have more options. They can then at least make a more informed decision about how they want to spend their money.

Children will inevitably make money mistakes. If you're paying close attention, you can capitalize on these mistakes and turn them into teachable moments. Help your child become more aware of how to manage money and how to stay in control.

## Teenagers and Money

By the time a child is a teenager, they will have many ideas about money. Some of these ideas, hopefully, will be empowered and smart; others, not so much. Teenagers seem naturally inclined to take risks in many areas of their life, including financially. Let's take a look at some tips and ideas to help your teenager manage their money more effectively, and responsibly.

**Get a Job** – It can be tough for teens to find jobs. The economy still isn't great in many areas. Additionally, they have school, sports, and other responsibilities. Babysitting gigs, mowing lawns, and summer jobs are all still an option. Getting a job helps them earn an income and that income needs to be managed and budgeted. It's a good experience.

**Technology woes** – Teens no longer handle much cash. They have a debit card to work with. If they're not careful, they can overspend and owe money to the bank in the form of bounced payments. Online shopping can cause problems too. Teach your teen that whether it's cash or credit, the money still comes from the same place – their bank account.

**The future is closer than you think** – Teens live in the moment. Next week is too far away, let alone next year or beyond. Help your teenager set money aside for after they graduate from high school. Even if their college will be paid for by scholarship, financial aid, or parents, it's always good to have extra cash just in case. Help them look beyond their next paycheck.

**Help them invest** – Teens are fully capable of starting an investment fund. Help them learn about stocks, bonds, and funds so that they can begin building a portfolio and leveraging their money. They may pout now but when they're in their twenties and thirties they'll be grateful for the money and the education.

**Talk about money** – Teens aren't great at their listening skills. However, they do hear you. Take time to talk about money. Leverage family budget meetings and other financial conversations to include your teen and help them get a big-picture idea of adult finances. They'll be adults before you know it and including them in the conversations can help them be prepared.

Teens will make money mistakes. As a parent, you can help them become more independent with their finances. Don't bail them out; instead allow them to learn, grow, and become smarter about money.

We've talked about teaching kids of all ages to become smarter about money. We've talked about budgeting, saving, spending, and donating money. These are all money values and to teach them, you have to be clear about your money values and priorities.

## Money Values to Consider

You have your own beliefs about money. These beliefs come from your parents, they come from your experience and they come from your knowledge about money. Your child will learn their money values from you. It's important to become clear about what you want them to learn. Your actions and words have an impact.

For example, imagine you're sitting at the kitchen table and you're paying bills and you say, "There's never enough." Your child hears this, and it can become part of their money language. Do you want them to have that attitude toward money or do you want something different for them?

**Get Clear on Your Beliefs about Money**

What's your money mindset? What thoughts do you have about money? What sayings do you find yourself repeating? For example, you may have grown up hearing, "Money doesn't grow on trees." Maybe you integrated that saying into your own life.

Write down or think about your beliefs and attitude toward money. Just because you find yourself saying something doesn't mean you believe it. Explore what you believe to be true about money and what you want your child to believe about money.

**Think about How You Can Model Your Beliefs**

What can you do when you're budgeting, talking about money and teaching your child about money that can support your beliefs? For example, if you want your child to believe that they can control their money and their financial situation then you can demonstrate that with positive comments about your budget and financial situation.

You can model your beliefs by being actively engaged in budgeting and managing your money. Your child will see this behaviour and embrace it as part of their own experience and belief system.

**What Values Do You Want Your Child to Have about Money?**

Finally, think about the values that you have about money and what you want your child to value. Some examples include:

1. **Saving** – Saving money for short-term goals, medium-term goals, and long-term goals. How can you model this value and help your child embrace saving?

1. **Giving** – Do you donate money to others? If so, what percentage of your income do you tithe? How can you model this value and teach your child to also donate some of their money or time to others?

3. **Materialism** – Children and adults both enjoy buying things. There's a balance between buying what you need and what you want. Teaching this balance is difficult. Think about your values on material goods and how you can model the values that you want your child to have.

Children will grow up with their thoughts, beliefs, and values about money. Empowering them now with skills and behaviours that support good money management will only strengthen their abilities as an adult. Identify what you believe about money, model that behaviour, and effectively teach your child to value money in a healthy and productive way.

Finally, because a bank account is part of the money management system that every child and adult needs to have, let's talk about bank accounts for every age of a child's life.

## Bank Accounts to Consider for Every Age

Bank accounts are part of managing your money. While you probably don't want to go out and get a checking account for your six-year-old, there are age-appropriate accounts. Let's look at some of your options.

**Elementary Age Children**

Christmas club accounts – This short-term savings account (less than 12 months) pays less than 2% interest. It's a good tool to begin teaching young children how to save.

Savings accounts – Children can have joint savings accounts with their parents. You can require your child to set aside a portion of cash gifts that they receive. You can open an account for them as soon as they're born and begin building savings for them. When they're old enough, you might consider transferring some of the money into a higher-yield investment account for college.

**Middle School Age Children**

**Savings account** – Your middle school-aged child may be able to manage a savings account with a debit card. At this age, you want to still be able to monitor their saving and spending. A joint account may still be in everyone's best interests. A debit card can begin to teach them about managing their money.

**Investment account** – If you don't have an investment account for your child yet, this can be a good time to introduce your child to stocks, bonds, and other investments. You can help them learn about investing and choose a good stock to start with.

**High School**

Checking Account – By high school, your child should be well on their way to becoming financially independent. That means having a checking account with a debit card and all of the responsibilities that come with it. Hopefully, they still have their savings account and an investment account too.

Banking is a part of managing your money. You can ease your child into the world of banking by starting them when they're young. By the time they're adults, they'll be well-versed in managing their money effectively.

Teaching your child about money isn't easy. It takes a careful plan. Opportunities present themselves in the form of your own financial decisions, your child's mistakes, and teachable moments outside the world. Children who learn to manage their money when they're young, are more likely to grow up being financially savvy and money smart.

CHAPTER SEVEN

# Teaching Children Moral Values

As stated before, you must instil a positive set of morals and values into your child if you want them to be successful and happy in the future. Many things in life will be much more difficult to accomplish without proper values if they can be done at all. Positive relationships will be much easier to build with proper moral values because your child will be more inclined to act in certain positive ways. Success will also be achieved much easier for a person with strong values compared to one who doesn't have. This is because the child with values will likely have a much better set of tools to use when making important decisions.

As you can see, moral values are very important for the development of your child. That is why it should be very high on your list of priorities and you should begin teaching them these values immediately. Before you can begin teaching your child morals and their importance, you must first understand the basics.

The following paragraphs will touch on the basics of morals and their importance for your child and the positive outcomes that teaching these values to your child will surely bring in the future.

**The Basics**

Morals and values can be taught in many different ways. In most cases, what works for one parent and child will most likely not produce the same results for a different parent and child. You have to explore and try different approaches.

If something does not work, it is time to try something else. There will be a lot of trial and error when it comes to raising your child. You must keep in mind that nobody is perfect and this includes parents. It may be difficult to continue looking for answers to help you get through to your child, but it is very important.

Your child depends on you for guidance in life. There are things you must do to make sure that they can live up to their full potential in the future. There are many benefits to instilling a positive set of morals and values into your child.

The following are some examples of the positive benefits that your child can receive from having good morals and values:

**Self-Respect:**

If your child is brought up with a positive set of morals and values, they will surely grow up to have healthy levels of self-respect and self-worth. This is because a child who has positive morals will make much more positive decisions than a child who does not. All of these positive decisions add up and the child will know that they make good decisions and that they are a good person. Self-respect contributes a great deal to the success of a child.

**Experience in School:**

Your child will most definitely have a better experience while attending school if they have good morals. They will be more responsible for their actions and not try to blame others for the things they do wrong. Their teachers will trust them more and will be more willing to work with them. You will notice that a lot of children with good morals like going to school because they understand the importance of it.

**Relationships:**

When your child reaches the age that it is time for them to start forming relationships, it will be much easier for them to function if they have a good set of morals. People will be much more inclined to be around a person that has a good set of morals and values than a person who does not. This is because people find it difficult to trust a person with poor values and morals and trust is needed in any relationship, whether personal or professional.

Fitting in with the other employees will be very difficult and the only people they will find who accept them will likely be other people with poor morals. Finding more people with poor morals will just lower their morals even more and reinforce their way of thinking. On the other hand, if you instil positive morals and values into your child they will attract others into their life who have the same set of beliefs. They will find much healthier relationships and will have many doors of opportunity open up for them. Good brings good and bad brings bad; so it is important to help your child be the best person they can be.

**Accountability:**

Children who have good morals are usually much more accountable than those who do not. That is why those who were brought up with good morals end up having much better relationships and opportunities in life. They do not pass blame, instead, they accept when they have done something wrong and try to do something to change it. This will also lead to much more trust between a parent and a child which is always healthy for a family relationship. This will make it easier for your child to talk to you, no matter what is on their mind, even if it means that they have to confess to something they have done.

**Be the Best Example**

Your child's mind can be thought of as a sponge. Everything around it gets absorbed. That is why it is important to make sure that your child has positive influences in their life. There should be one main role model, however, and that is your job as a parent. It is important to understand that your child develops a lot of their behaviours from what they see you do. It's as the saying goes, "monkey see monkey do".

You need to make sure that you are constantly setting a positive example for your child. Your child thinks that you are a superhero and that you know the right way to do everything, which is why you must act like a superhero and always be positive.

The following paragraphs will shed some light on the importance of being a good example as a parent and how you can do so.

**Be a Superhero**

As mentioned above, you must act like a superhero around your child. I do not mean that you need to go out at night in a mask and cape and go out and fight armed criminals. I mean that you need to always do the right thing in every situation, no matter how difficult it may be or what rewards a negative decision may offer you. By doing this you will show your child that it is important to always do the right thing.

You must lead by example. It is much more likely that your child will pick up on the lessons being provided when they are taught by example and not just from the things that you say. This is especially true when parents try to tell their children not to do something because it is bad. You must understand that it is difficult for a child to wrap their mind around this concept. For example, many parents tell their children not to smoke cigarettes because they are unhealthy and can kill, while the entire time they have a lit cigarette hanging out of their mouth. This message will surely not be retained as the child will think nothing of it after watching their parents do exactly what they were telling them not to do. The same goes for teaching your child morals; you must practice what you preach!

You need to determine what morals you need to teach your child and find ways that you can demonstrate these morals by example. For example, if you want your child to learn to be kind, you may help an elder neighbour carry in their groceries or help them trim their lawn at no charge. Another way you can show this moral value is to give to a charity or provide a meal to someone in need. If you want to teach your child about being accountable you must take responsibility for everything that is your fault, no matter how small you may think the issue is or how bad the outcome may be.

This will teach your child to not fear the consequences of being honest and to be more accountable for their decisions in life. If you want your child to learn responsibility, you may want to try taking them to work with you for a day so they can see all the responsibilities that you have daily. You may also want to have a talk with them about the responsibilities in the life of paying the bills and making sure that there is always food on the table. This will help them understand that life is not one big game and will prepare them for the day that they must become responsible for their own life.

What you need to do is determine which moral values your child may be lacking or which morals you would like to change about your child and create a game plan. Your efforts may not work at first and may take some time to show progress but you will surely be successful in your efforts if you try hard enough. One of the most important things you need to do is analyse your morals and values and make sure you are exhibiting positive lessons as a parent.

**Begin Teaching Young**

You mustn't wait until the later stages of a child's life to begin teaching them positive morals and values and how important they are to live. This is something that must be done as soon as possible. You may think that your child is too young to understand lessons about morals and values, but this is not true. Children understand much more than many people think they do and begin retaining information from a very early age.

Begin teaching your child the importance of morals and values at a very early age. Your efforts will be much more beneficial if you do so.

**The Sooner the Better**

Many parents make the mistake of waiting until a child's later stages in the development process before they take action on the moral standards of their child. This is a big mistake and I will tell you why. By the time a child is in the later stages of their development, they already have a mind of their own. It is much harder to shape a child's mind when they are older.

The more they grow, the more free will they acquire. They will eventually get to the point that they do not want to listen to what you have to say and would rather make their own decisions and learn their life lessons. This can have very negative consequences because the child will not want to listen to someone who knows things from experience and will likely make foolish decisions. If you start at a very early age, your child's brain is like a sponge, as mentioned previously.

Scientific studies have shown that a large amount of your child's development begins in the first five years of their life. Now, do you see why it is so important to begin teaching your child at a young age?

There are many ways that you can teach your child positive morals and values at an early age. A few examples are provided below:

**Give Them Responsibilities:**

Provide your child with some responsibilities around the house. Sitting around watching TV or playing video games all day will have no positive influence on their morals.

Your child must have duties that they need to do every day, even if they are small responsibilities. A couple of examples may be cleaning up their messes or making their bed in the morning. You will likely be surprised by how much difference these little responsibilities make in your child's morals.

**Hold Them Accountable:**

You must hold your child accountable for their actions. You also need to understand that children will be children. It is important to find a healthy balance between leniency and being strict. Some parents let their children get away with entirely too much without any sort of discipline.

They try to be the child's friend and not their parent which leads to the child thinking that there are no real consequences for any of their actions in life. This will have very negative consequences for them and will likely lead to their not reaching their full potential in life.

On the other hand, if you are too strict you will not make a positive impact on your child either. They will likely begin to ignore you because they do not feel close to you and will hide things from you and lie to you because of fear of punishment.

**Honesty is the Best Policy:**

Your child must understand, even from a very early age, that lying is never good under any circumstances. If your child lies to you there needs to be some sort of discipline. Be careful when selecting your method of discipline though because you do not want to be too stern with your child. Another thing that you may want to avoid is entertaining made-up stories. Imagination is one thing but if a child is making stories up to get out of something there is a problem that needs to be addressed.

**Volunteer Work:**

Volunteer work is a great way for a child to learn very important morals for life. Even at a very early age, some volunteer associations will allow children to help them with their volunteer work. An example that you may want to consider would be your child making sandwiches in a food drive for the needy. Another example might be to serve food in a food kitchen on a holiday. This will teach your child to appreciate what they have and to not be greedy with things in life. It will also teach your child to be kind and compassionate in life and provide them with the capability of loving others as they love themselves.

**Pay Attention**

In today's society, there are many negative things all around that can negatively impact your child and their set of morals and values. Everywhere you look there is something negative or violent going on. The streets are filled with chaos and the media is filled with violence.

Music is full of hate and video games are full of drug use. What can you do to protect your child from all the external factors that you do not want to influence your child? The answer is simple, you have to spend time with them and pay attention to what is going on in their life.

**Get Involved**

Numerous things in life can negatively influence your child. The most important thing you can do to help your child avoid these negative influences is to get involved in their life.

You need to know what is going on with them and the types of situations and influences that exist in their life. Your child may make it seem sometimes like you are spying on them or not letting them live their own life. You must ignore this because you must be involved in your child's life.

The following are some examples of things you need to be aware of and things you need to avoid if you want your child to develop a good set of morals and values:

**Know Your Child's Friends:**

Children can easily be influenced by other children. In some cases, a child will listen to another child more than an adult. That is why it is extremely important for you as a parent to know who your children associate with.

If your child has negative influences as friends, their moral standing may be in jeopardy. Even if your child does not agree with what a certain individual is doing, they may eventually begin to participate anyway because they want to gain the acceptance of that person; this is only human nature. The more that your child engages in these activities the less bad they will feel about it. This will lead to changes in your child's morals and values and things they used to think were not good suddenly. This could include drug use, lying, stealing, or other negative behaviours.

**Watch Out for Certain Video Games:**

Video games are becoming increasingly violent. On top of that, they are also starting to promote drug and alcohol use and other types of behaviours more and more. The problem with a child playing games such as these is that a child can have difficulties distinguishing what is good in a video game and what is good in real life.

This leads to children doing some very shocking things. There have been instances where children have been seriously hurt or have hurt or even killed other children. When they were asked why they did what they did, they would reply that it was seen in their video game and that they didn't think that anyone would get hurt.

Situations such as these happen a lot more than you probably think. This is the main reason why there are ratings on video game covers. Parents need to stop buying video games that are meant for people ages 17+ for young children. There is a reason why those games have mature ratings.

They are not meant for minds that can be moulded as easily as a child's. Parents like to try to blame video games for their child's actions, but they should be asking themselves why they bought them for their children in the first place.

**Music:**

Just like other forms of media, music can either be beneficial for your child's morals or can be completely negative. Often, it is negative. You need to know what type of music your child listens to. In years before iPads and iPhones, your child would listen to their music on their stereo, and you would be able to hear what they were listening to. In today's age, children are always walking around with earphones in and you have no idea what they are listening to.

Take a minute to ask your child who some of their favourite musicians are and ask them if you can listen to some of their music with them sometimes. You must ask if you can listen with them and not on your own because this will let your child know that you are interested and not just trying to pry into their life.

**Free Time:**

You also need to know what your child is doing with their free time. If you are trying to boost your child's moral standards, it would be a good idea to consider placing your child in some extra-curricular activities. These activities will teach your child responsibility and how to be accountable for their actions. This is very important for the development of a healthy set of morals and values.

**Keep Communication Open**

It's important that your child feels as if they can talk to you about anything. This will promote them, to be always honest and to be accountable for their actions. This is very important if you want your child to grow up to have a strong foundation provided by moral values. Keeping an open line of communication with your child will surely make many situations that will arise in their future much easier to cope with and handle.

It is important to keep in mind that this may not always be because you will most likely hear things that you do not want to hear over time. You must stay cool-headed as well as calm and collected or this will never help your child's morals.

The following paragraphs will go over the benefits of being open with your child as well as some challenges you should be expecting to face.

### The Benefits of Being Open

Many benefits can be offered by being open with your child. You mustn't be selective with what you can be open with your child about. Having discussions with your child about issues they are facing or things that they may be thinking of doing can provide great opportunities for you as a parent to instil morals into them. Children naturally look for guidance; it is how we as humans work. You must positively offer that guidance.

These discussions can offer many positive moral influences to your child. It will teach them to be accountable for their actions. It will teach them right from wrong. It will teach them about sticking to their goals. One of the most important things it will teach them is to have integrity and be honest no matter what the consequences are.

You need to know you have to do half of the work in this process. It is also important that you are aware of the fact that you will likely hear things that upset or disappoint you while you have an open relationship with your child.

You must keep your head together if you want this process to work. If you cannot appropriately react to a situation you are neither helping your child nor giving them a positive example of how to handle their issues in the future. No matter what you hear, you have to approach it with a level head.

You have to remember and appreciate the fact that your child is coming to you for guidance. As much as something angers you, you mustn't speak to your child like you are mad at them. You must show that you understand and while you do not have to like the discussion you must respect them for coming to you.

It will help this process greatly if you show your child that they are building trust with you by being open with you. Give them a little bit more privileges or let them do a few things you couldn't trust them to do before, such as staying out late with friends or borrowing the family car.

**Point Out Good Values and Choices**

If you want your child to truly understand the value of good morals and all the benefits that they will bring to their life, you must point out the good choices that your child makes in life. Some parents make the mistake of only pointing out the things that their child is not doing correctly. This is a bad habit and, understandably, they may not know another way of parenting, but they need to learn another way quickly.

You need to make a big deal when your child makes correct decisions in life, especially when it comes to big decisions. This will reinforce their behaviours and make them want to hold on to the morals that you have tried to raise them with.

**Point Out the Positives**

Pointing out or paying attention to nothing but the negative things a child does or the wrong decision that they make can be very damaging to their self-image. This can put a child in danger of losing their morals and values and developing new ones that are negative instead of positive. Children naturally seek their parent's approval, so continuously focusing on a child's wrongdoings can make the child feel as if they are not a good person or are not good enough for you. You do not want your child to feel this way as it will almost surely destroy their future.

You need to reinforce every positive decision your child makes with their life, no matter how small of a decision it is. Positively reinforcing behaviour is an almost guaranteed way to keep that behaviour continuing. Whether it be that your child got straight A's on their report card or decided to do their homework before playing video games, you need to make sure that you acknowledge it and make sure that they know that you know what they have done.

You may want to set up a reward system that is designed around building the moral character of your child. For their smaller achievements along their journey, you may offer them a small reward. When your child achieves a larger goal they should be treated to a larger reward. Remember, their rewards do not always have to be material objects. You may want to steer clear of rewarding your child with material objects as much as possible. Using material objects can make a child develop a habit of expecting a reward every time they do something. Instead offer rewards such as later bedtimes, friends staying over, or allowing them to spend more time on their video game system that day.

The most difficult part in all of this is most likely the fact that you have to learn how to be balanced. Just as you cannot only focus on the negatives of a child, you cannot only focus on the positives either. Children are, after all, just children.

They need guidance and will make wrong decisions from time to time. It is important that you hold your child accountable for their actions and not make excuses for them if you want them to have a good set of morals and values. When your child does something wrong you need to point it out. Not only will it be beneficial for the morals of your child, but it will also be appreciated by your child.

Children want to feel the structure. The structure is how children know that you care for them. The fact that you do not let them do whatever they like shows them that you love them, even if they do not act like it at the time.

The most important fact to remember while trying to build your child's moral standards is that you are the parent. You will have to have difficult conversations and do difficult things, but it is all for the benefit of your child.

# Conclusion

It is understandable for you to look at the task of instilling a good set of values into your child as a very difficult journey. However, it does not need to be. By being a good role model and being involved in your child's life, you will be doing a lot to ensure that your child grows up with a good set of values. One of the most important things you can do is simply show your child that you care and the importance of being a good person. You can do that, can't you?

The information that you have read in this book should be very helpful for you when it comes to teaching your child morals and values. Just apply what you have learned, and you should begin to see improvements in their character in no time at all.

Printed by Libri Plureos GmbH in Hamburg,
Germany